THE CRISIS IN CHINA

BY LIEUT.-COLONEL

P. T. ETHERTON

LATE H.M. CONSUL-GENERAL IN CHINESE TURKESTAN
AND ADDITIONAL ASSISTANT JUDGE OF H.M. SUPREME
COURT FOR CHINA

Author of "Across the Roof of the World,"
"In the Heart of Asia"

"Armies can be found ; a leader is difficult."
CHINESE PROVERB

BOSTON
LITTLE, BROWN, AND COMPANY
1927

MADE AND PRINTED IN GREAT BRITAIN BY
BILLING AND SONS, LTD., GUILDFORD AND ESHER

A SECTION OF THE GREAT WALL

It runs across China from the Yellow Sea to the Far West.

PREFACE

IN the following pages I have endeavoured to allow the facts of the present situation in China to speak for themselves, without presenting a case for any of the Powers or parties concerned.

China is in a state of transition to which the history of the world can offer no parallel. The evolution now in progress affects not only British policy and trade, but has a direct bearing on the future of the Pacific, and of those Powers whose interests lie in that region.

In so far as we personally are concerned, the studied moderation of the British Government, in face of threat and outrage, should convince even the most rabid partisans of Canton that Great Britain is a powerful friend, whom the China of to-morrow would find helpful and sympathetic in the task that confronts the Chinese nation of evolving order from chaos, of establishing a government that is, both in its inspiration and aims, truly national and imbued with the ideals at present lacking. As will be seen it is an immense undertaking, demanding a leader of genius, with cordial and whole-hearted co-operation, which is not easy to obtain in a land so peculiarly constituted as China.

It is in the interests of ourselves and the whole world that China should progress to ordered government and prosperity ; it is also essential, in view of what is involved in the present crisis, that the points at issue should be more generally known than is the case at present. If this book enables the reader to form a considered opinion of the potential consequences of the Chinese crisis, it will have served its purpose.

In the preparation of the book I desire to place on record my appreciation of the assistance given me by Mr. H. Hessell Tiltman and of criticism and advice which he has so readily accorded.

P. T. ETHERTON.

LONDON.
April, 1927.

CONTENTS

Contents

CHAPTER VIII

EXTRA-TERRITORIALITY AND CUSTOMS

CHAPTER IX

CHINA AND THE FAR EAST

CHAPTER X

THE FUTURE OF CHINA

LIST OF ILLUSTRATIONS

xiii

CHINA: ITS PRESENT EXTENT

CHINA: THE FACTS

CHAPTER I

ITS PRESENT EXTENT

NAPOLEON is credited with the saying that it is in Asia that the destinies of Europe will one day be decided. Certain it is that the Far East has always been a bone of contention between rival European Powers, while China is in a definite stage of transition, and is absorbing world-wide attention. Since the revolution following the overthrow of the monarchy in 1911, and particularly within the past two years, events on the Chinese stage have moved with kaleidoscopic rapidity, fresh factions have risen from day to day, new warring elements have joined in the scramble for power and loot, and leaders have succeeded one another in lightning succession, until the general public the world over has become lost in the bewildering maze of military governors, war lords, and rival aspirants and governments for supremacy. Within a space of fourteen years forty-three governments have been set up and deposed in Peking, eight Presidents have come and gone, and China now finds herself without a central ruling authority, and exposed to civil and internecine warfare on a vast scale—a nation without a Government.

To gain a clear grasp of the situation, and form an opinion as to the near future, it is essential to explain what the so-called Republic of China comprises, with a comparative statement of its former extent under the monarchy. No limit can be placed to the importance of China as a factor in world affairs ; its population totals a quarter of the human race, with an area of four and a quarter million square miles.

As at present constituted, there are twenty-two organised provinces and the dependencies of Mongolia, Tibet, and Kokonor, but the first two are only nominally under China. Despite the appointment of a Chinese Resident at Lhasa, the land of the lamas is ruled by a theocratic Government, with the Dalai Lama as the political, and the Tashilumpo Lama as the ecclesiastical, head.

A reference to the map will show the location of the provinces and the three principal rivers that divide the country into three sections. Firstly, the Yangtse rises in the Kuen Lun Mountains of Tibet, flows for 3,200 miles through China and touches nine of the provinces. This river is the real heart of China, and drains some 700,000 square miles, the principal cities along its banks being Hankow and Nanking, with Shanghai at the mouth.

North of the Yangtse is the Hoang Ho, or Yellow River, which, although commercially not so important, has the glamour of sanctity over its outflow to the Yellow Sea in Shantung, being the Holy Land of China and birthplace of Confucius, whose teachings have dominated Chinese life and thought for twenty-five centuries.

The third largest river is the Si Kiang, or West River in the South, with Canton, the oldest port in China, at its mouth. Canton has been prominent in foreign trade since the third century B.C., whilst it was the first Celestial port visited by European craft, the earliest English ship touching there in 1637.

Prior to the revolution of 1911, the land throughout the Empire was, theoretically, the property of the Emperor, who could dispose of it as he wished; the mountains, the deserts, the valleys and the plains, all belonged to him; indeed, he was regarded as the Son of Heaven since, according to Chinese conception, he ruled over all beneath the sun, and as late as 1860 could only treat with foreign nations on the basis of inferiority, and their doing obeisance to him as the paramount power in the Universe. Moreover, the Emperor was revered as the father of the nation, this being the model on which the government of the country was based, as expounded by Confucius, who declared the well-ordered and well-regulated family to be the finest conception of how a country should be governed. It was the crux of the old system of government, and to appreciate the full significance and influence it has exerted throughout the centuries to the present day we must note that Chinese family life is in direct opposition to that of Europe. With us the children are under parental control only until they are of age, in many cases not even up to that stage, when they separate and form households of their own. The Chinese son, however, remains part and parcel of the establishment, irrespective of marriage, and parental authority over him undergoes no modification. This is the tie that binds all together, so that the family was the real starting-point in the government and constitution of the country. The Emperor as head of the nation was responsible to Heaven, whose representative he was on earth, whilst the governors of provinces, sub-governors, prefects, and district magistrates, were in turn answerable to their immediate superiors. Then came the people, the head of a family being ruler over his juniors, with authority in all that concerned estates and property, responsible only for his actions and misdeeds to his ancestors, whence emanated his mandate of headship, and to whom he offered prayers as the family priest.

Mencius, the sage who followed Confucius and emphasised the vital import of the latter's teaching, gave it as a canon of social and political life that the people and the family were the national mainstay, that they should rank first, the gods and the monarch to follow in order of precedence. The Chinese philosophers recognised that the people should be given full recognition in accordance with the Confucian dictate, and that explains the wide personal liberty and freedom of the subject which are so jealously guarded in China. Incidentally it also explains why the doctrines of Bolshevism are at variance with Chinese life and thought in matters of private liberty and private trade.

Although unrestricted personal liberty does not exist as such in any country of the world, it has probably attained a higher level in China than elsewhere. Even the wild tribes of the jungle and the desert have manners and customs by which their individual liberties and

SHANTUNG

Kufu : The tomb of Confucius in the cemetery which covers more than 500 acres, and where repose the bones of the Confucian clan in all its branches for the past 2,500 years.

activities are curtailed. But we can go a step further
and note how the law of the jungle applies to wild
animals, how complete freedom of action is hedged
around with limitations, and the wolf, for instance, acts
under the guidance and instructions of his leader, until
that leader, either through old age or failure to assert
his authority, succumbs to another, younger and more
virile than he who has gone before.

The essence of civilisation is the surrender to Society
of individual freedom in constantly increasing measure.
The institution of private property postulates such a
measure, while the recognition of property rights in land
involves the complete negation of the theory that man
possesses freedom to tread the soil. We shall see later
on how these remarks apply with peculiar force to the
Chinese nation.

This liberty of the subject is all-important, for it
extends to the humblest of Celestial subjects, and
although wars and upheavals may come and go, and
strife be rampant throughout the land, they do not affect
these principles, and in dealing with the Chinese question
should be constantly borne in mind as a dominant factor.
This freedom in normal times is highly developed, and
there is little or no call upon the Chinese subject as we
understand the term. He may move about without let
or hindrance, may establish his trade or profession
wherever it suits him ; there are no regulations so made
to restrain excess in food, clothing, or any luxuries, and
municipal law is unknown.

One of the vital questions as between European nations
and the Chinese at the moment is the question of extra-

territoriality, and the revision of the Chinese code of law, with a view to bringing it into line with that of Western Powers, and so justify us in handing over British subjects to the mercy of a Chinese court. The penal code, sound in wording but weak in application, is the only law that exists as a State institution, and even that is only applied in cases of necessity, the principles enunciated by Confucius being generally adhered to in a settlement. No oath is administered in a court of law, as the Chinese, apart from the difficulty of formulating one acceptable to the Celestial mind, do not believe that an oath will induce the accused, the witness, or whoever it may be, to tell the truth if he is inclined to do otherwise. Here again we must realise that lying, as such, is not a disgrace, and to save himself, to appear well before the world, and preserve inviolate his position, honour, and reputation, he will lie quite cheerfully, and none will think any the worse of him. If he has preserved "face," to quote the Chinese expression—the most powerful and far-reaching expression in the language, and one that the people put above all else—all is well ; but if, on the contrary, he has failed, disgrace is by universal verdict his lot.

Naturally there are ways and means of circumventing the law and saving one's face. I had an example of this in a case brought before the local magistrate, in which a merchant of standing was accused of complicity in the opium traffic. For him to have been beaten, or undergone any form of punishment, would have entailed a loss of face that could never be retrieved, so drastic action was indicated—a substitute must be procured.

This is not a formidable problem, for in every Chinese town and village there are men whose livelihood is gained by serving terms of punishment or receiving the strokes awarded to another. It will be seen that bribery and corruption are rife in China, and no one is immune from their operation. So the merchant secured the man he was in search of, the police in turn were approached, and negotiations made it worth their while to meta-phorically look the other way. The case came up for hearing and was duly disposed of, justice was done—at any rate, by proxy—and the world went on as before. Doubtless a percentage of the money that passed eventually found its way into the pocket of the district magistrate, who had originally purchased his appoint-ment for so many thousand taels. He would be, after all, merely recovering that amount by degrees, and he would be regarded as an anomaly if he did other-wise.

The Chinese are essentially a peace-loving and law-abiding people, always anxious to avoid coming into contact with the law. Should they be involved, money is at once their first appeal and the means by which they may extricate themselves from an odious situation. It follows that the rich man has an easy course ; the law in his case has few, if any, terrors, provided he uses his financial resources with a liberal hand. That is the easier and more advantageous course, although Western nations have suggested that Chinese courts should have advo-cates on both sides, as with us, but the Celestial regards their employment from a totally different standpoint, fails to perceive any advantage arising from them, implying that the obvious course is the one dictated by money.

In a study of the Chinese question, as presented to the world to-day, one is apt to lose sight of the fact that ninety-seven per cent. of the Chinese people are illiterate, and that of the remaining three per cent. very few concern themselves with politics and what is passing in the great world beyond their own frontiers. Confucius counselled all to concern themselves only with their own affairs, and that he who meddles with politics places himself in a dangerous position. So, with wars and revolutions and all that is happening in China notwithstanding, we are still confronted with the Chinese nation as a whole, who are little affected by present events, and still follow the even tenor of their ways, the identical course laid down centuries before the birth of Christ.

With the prevalent and widespread anarchy and chaos, local and municipal government have passed through varying phases of change and application, according to the particular war lord and his methods in any given area. This has not, however, vitally affected the government of the people; the old-time principles remain constant, and it is only in taxation, forced contributions, and anticipation of revenue, that changes have been introduced.

We have seen that the social organisation is based on the family, and the advent of the Republic and institution of Parliamentary methods have not materially altered the leading features of local administration. For governmental purposes the twenty-two provinces are divided into divisions and districts, the former under an

official called "taoyin," the latter being the district
chief and chief police authority in his area.

The district magistrate is the one who comes into
direct contact with the people, and his functions are
comprehensive. He is the real ruler of the people, his
duties embodying matters touching on law, education,
trade, and everything that affects directly and indirectly
the welfare of the masses. There is probably no official
in any country the scope of whose duties is at once so
wide and far-reaching. In a suit before his court he is
judge and jury, responsible for law and order throughout his district, and is in charge of the police and system
of protection as known in a Chinese town. He supervises
the collection of taxes, is in charge of public works, roads,
canals, and bridges within his area, keeps an eye upon
the temples and the priests to whose care they are
nominally confided, and in cases of local distress, such
as drought or famine, will conduct the intercessional
services and himself head the procession to the temple
of the gods, clad in sackcloth and ashes and equipped
with numerous joss-sticks to be ignited before the deity.

Often the districts are as large as Yorkshire, and, to
place him in closer touch with the people, headmen of
villages are appointed, with a chief over every ward
into which towns are divided. To all intents and purposes
these headmen exercise complete control, and have wide
powers in the disposal of small cases, the right to grant
residence within the ward, or to withhold it from doubtful
characters, whom he can eject without reference to the
law. This system leads to extensive corruption and black-
mail, but he is usually careful not to overstep the mark,

since there is always the danger that he may fall foul of his superior through intrigue or as the result of undue pressure upon the people of his ward for personal gain.

Public opinion is almost unknown in China ; a public spirit does not exist, although a form of it is apparent where the work of the magistrate is concerned, which he cannot ignore, as it may react against him. His salary is entirely inadequate for even immediate needs ; the governmental system does not provide for that, and he is expected to make his own arrangements. The yield of the district over which he rules is known within a couple of thousand taels or so, the revenue to be submitted to the central authority being gauged accordingly. So long as that amount is produced, and the people do not murmur in the process of collection, no inquiries are made as to the original levy, and he is at liberty to squeeze his district, provided that law and order and the regular remission of a stated sum to the central Treasury are not jeopardised.

As already remarked, the district magistrate renders no account of receipt and expenditure ; there is no system of accounts in any of the provinces which would not need in turn to be checked.

Above the district magistrates is the ''taoyin,'' or prefect, with a number of districts committed to his charge, varying with the area and importance of the province. He is a general administrator, supervisor of Customs and revenue, and an important official from the international standpoint, for he is the pivot on which all provincial business turns.

Above the taoyin is the provincial governor, assisted
by a number of officials for the various departments of
finance, justice, trade, and administration generally. In
turn the governor is responsible to the central authority—
when such exists—and, despite the prevailing disorder,
the Republican administration is almost identical with
that under the Empire.

Since a large number of officials still hold office
awarded to them under the old régime, and the ranks
of the Civil Service were, until within recent years, filled
by competitive examination, it will be of interest to outline this remarkable system, the main plank in the
monarchical government of China. Education is a great
point with the Chinese. The Confucian dictum has it
that you should rear pigs rather than children if they
are not given a sound education, and thus it exercises
widespread influence on public questions, and will in
the future play a leading part in the reformation of a
country where there has ever been respect for learning.
True, its pursuit is largely confined to the *literati,* but
it is none the less revered, and the scholar is still regarded
as the leading light of the community. The civil and
military officials were entirely recruited from them, their
ranks were open to all, however poor, who had literary
aspirations, and the system certainly afforded an equality
of opportunity which in theory, at any rate, was sound.
This method of selection served the general ends of
political equity, and was a stabilising factor in the
government of the country.

The syllabus of the examinations was based on the
ancient classics, a knowledge of which was essential

down to the smallest detail. From Tibet to Manchuria, and Canton to Peking, the classics of Confucius and Mencius were the sheet anchor ; the doctrines enunciated in them were to be followed, more particularly the advantage of moral over physical force, or the application of right over might. Confucius urged the necessity of appointing only the most competent to rule, and he favoured the deposition of even an emperor, should he be weighed in the balance and found wanting. This system had many results, but none more potent than the type of mentality it produced and the standard of thought and practice evolved, to which no other country can offer a parallel.

Education as thus exploited held the people together and was peculiarly suited to the Chinese temperament. With Western influence and the advance of modern ideas of thought and government, drastic changes will eventuate in China, since the problems of to-day cannot be determined by reference to the classics ; new methods and a revised form of learning and education are demanded, enabling the Chinese official to cope with modern questions. A new type of scholar is indicated, for, as Bacon says, we should study reason and experience and not confine ourselves to the books of the ancients, a forceful argument that is appealing to the modern Chinese scholar. This new factor in Celestial evolution is slowly beginning to realise that he must study the entire world as to fact and application.

As regards the competitive examinations held in China, there were three degrees, the first being attained by possibly one per cent. of the candidates. In the second degree there were often ten thousand candidates for sixty vacancies, and the third or higher degree might yield a thousand from the whole empire as the product of the eliminating tests.

The final examination was held in Peking, the candidates comprising all those who had survived the trials at the various provincial capitals. The examination halls in Peking numbered ten thousand cells, each about five feet by three, and of corresponding height, light and necessaries being admitted through a grating. The candidate was thoroughly searched before entry to insure that he carried nothing that would assist him in the coming ordeal. Enclosed by those narrow cells, the flower of Chinese literary talent grappled with abstruse problems and matters of political and judicial import as propounded by the sages five centuries before the birth of Christ. There the candidate was left for days on end, the questions being such that many of the more highly strung went mad under the strain, since the slightest mistake in composition, or the misplacing of a character, meant disaster. But this was not all, for if he aspired to the super-degree he must appear at an examination conducted by the Emperor in person. The number was limited to three hundred and twenty, these representing the cream of the *literati* and the product of years of the most intense study. From them a dozen might be chosen to receive the highest appointments such as viceroy of a province, with all the reward and kudos that it carried in its wake. When we realise there are several thousand characters in the Chinese classics, many of them containing from twenty to thirty dots and strokes, the slightest deviation in which alters the meaning of a phrase, the mental strain imposed can be imagined.

We will now follow the fortunes of a successful candidate promoted to a district magistracy. His authority was limited by the Confucian teachings, and kept in check by the adoption of rules which were the outcome of experience and the reasoning of a practically minded people. For instance, no official could hold office within the province of his birth, this being designed to guard against local interests growing up to compete with duty, and against any territorial attachment which might become the basis of disloyalty and lead to trouble and the fomenting of disorder.

The tenure of appointment was for three years, this rule being generally adhered to, although I have known instances where the official has continued to hold office for seven years and more, when it was to the advantage of those above him that he should do so. With this rule in vogue there was slight opportunity to establish personal influence, or to unduly assert himself in his district.

On arrival there he would be a comparative stranger, and largely dependent upon his personal staff in the discharge of magisterial duties. His salary would be negligible ; the district, as already seen, must supply that deficiency, and from this can be traced the course of bribery and corruption. Li Hung Chang, one of the greatest statesmen China has ever produced, once said that the value of any appointment was in direct proportion to the money that could be made out of it, and from that frank statement we arrive at the underlying principles of government. To reach his present position the district magistrate will have had to make expensive presents ; probably he has borrowed heavily at usurious rates to enable him to pursue his studies and to purchase his outfit when he has been declared successful, and all this must be repaid. That truism carries us to the methods of taxation, which, although evolved from long usage, are still in force and follow the empirical principle of being levied where there is promise of a good yield. The land and grain taxes are the most important, since seventy-four per cent. of the population are agricultural, and the revenue resulting therefrom is a considerable item.

The land tax varies according to extent and productivity, the assessments having been in some cases drawn up generations ago. Provided the tax on land has been paid for a period of three years without default, it is the title to ownership. There are other taxes, such as that on salt, and sundry octroi duties, but no municipal levy, water, or poor rates. As a class the Chinese nation is lightly assessed—apart from the abnormal exactions and oppression now going on under the numerous provincial war lords—and they respond to the calls made upon them with cheerfulness, and even with enthusiasm in certain circumstances. This was exemplified in the Tai-ping Rebellion of 1863, when, to repair the damage wrought by that upheaval, and restock the depleted Imperial Treasury, the people voluntarily imposed a tax known to this day as the "likin," being one-tenth per cent. on all sales. It was primarily a military levy and approved only as a temporary measure. However, it is still in force as one of the principal taxes of the empire, giving considerable trouble to foreign merchants, and especially their consuls, by its interference with trade and the disputes arising from it.

Land is specified as first, second, and third grade, and is more or less accurate, and the measuring chains rigid or elastic in proportion to the amount of silver dust cast in the eyes of the surveyors. In addition to those afforded by the land and grain taxes, there are various methods for the acquisition of wealth. For instance, the military authorities lodge a demand for wood to meet specific requirements. The local official, to whom the collection of the fuel is confided, summons his subordinates, who are sent forth to arrange for the supply at the existing market rate. The requisitioning proceeds apace, and to such an extent is the area swept of wood that the price has risen to three or four times its original figure. The people then represent to the magistrate that any further commandeering can only result in hardship; so the latter assumes a benevolent air, and notifies that, such being the case, he will not insist upon the full amount being delivered, but will accept the amount outstanding in cash at the prevailing market price, now four times higher than it stood when the requisitioning commenced.

The same principles apply to the grain tax collected after the harvest, the taxpayers attending at the local receipt of Customs with their quota of cereals. If, however, by bringing that amount they consider themselves freed from further obligation, they will be grievously disappointed. Ordinarily the official scales give comparatively correct measure, but when it comes to an

THE SUMMER PALACE, PEKING

THE TEMPLE OF HEAVEN, PEKING

adjustment of the grain tax it is extraordinary the amount that is required to induce them to obey the laws of gravity.

China is, by authorities well qualified to speak, regarded as the richest country on earth, and the yield from even light taxation, were it properly levied and accounted for, would be colossal. What can be effected in this way is exemplified in the operations of the Imperial Maritime Customs, formed by the genius of Sir Robert Hart, who assumed control in 1863, and during his fifty-four years of service in China made it a model of efficiency, coupled with a maximum yield. Originally the receipts from this source were divided between Peking and the provinces, but with the fall of the Manchu régime in 1911 it was diverted to the redemption of foreign debt. This foreign debt only arose in China after the war with Japan, the Maritime Customs being used as the security for the financial assistance received, which help from foreign sources has gone on increasing until the indebtedness now exceeds approximately £200,000,000.

Having dealt with the system of administration, we will pass in brief review the religions of China—Confucianism, Taoism, and Buddhism. The first has never been given the character of an established religion, but rather a code of social and political doctrines, which, as President Yuan Shih Kai once expressed it, is held most sacred by the entire Chinese people. He was emphatic on the necessity of preserving the traditional beliefs of China ; indeed, he was partly in favour of making it the State religion under the Republic. Some felt that it was

3

putting back the clock to recognise any form of belief, but Yuan pointed out that he merely wished to make a strong point of the moral and ethical principles of Confucianism as a basis of education, the more so as there was no connection with myth or theology in the proposal.

The worship of their ancestors is prominent in the religious and social life of the Chinese people ; it is the one influence that dominates all classes of Society, and none dares neglect the worship of those who have gone before. To propitiate them, to merit their assistance and goodwill, and to insure the prosperity of the family is a bounden duty, otherwise disaster will attend failure to discharge those obligations. At stated intervals in the year offerings are made to the spirits of ancestors, feasts are given, and when the festivities terminate the Celestial has no further dread of evil spirits, nor will ill-luck befall his crops, cattle, or affairs.

The next religion—that of Taoism—is the development of a philosophy enunciated by a sage called Lao Tzu, but, as seen to-day in China, it is a depraved form of worship in which demons and witchcraft play the leading part. Finally, there comes Buddhism, with its fascinating ritual as propounded by the Buddha, which really supplanted the erstwhile glories of Taoism. Buddhism was introduced from India just before the Christian era, but, although it spread over a large part of China, it never supplanted the position that Confucius holds in the estimation of the people.

So much for the religions of China, and in the next chapter we will deal with the social side of Chinese life.

THE CHINESE AT HOME

CHAPTER II

THE CHINESE AT HOME

IT is not within the scope of this book to discuss at any length Chinese social life or Celestial manners and customs, but an insight into the national character is essential before we can deal with the points at issue, on the outcome of which the psychology of the Chinese temperament will largely operate.

It has been shown that theoretically the empire was ruled by an autocratic monarch responsible to Heaven, whose representative he was over all beneath the skies, and the precepts and principles inculcated during the past four thousand years have created certain definite lines of thought and action that must be borne in mind in any review of the actual situation. In November, 1913, the first President of the Republic declared in a decree promulgated in Peking that the entire Chinese people hold most sacred the doctrines and teachings of Confucius, and he was convinced of the necessity of preserving inviolate the traditional Chinese beliefs.

We have seen that three-quarters of the population are agricultural, and the Republican Government recognised the danger of neglecting the worship of Heaven, for the agrarian element being so strong and conservative is a formidable factor that must always be reckoned with, and evolution is slow in China.

As already remarked, the family is the social unit, Chinese writers asserting that this must be the basis of sound government and the one under which prosperity will be readily obtained. Of all nations the Chinese are probably the most domesticated in the world, with a real and abiding affection for the home, the land of their birth, and the particular town or village from which they originate. Large numbers of Chinese emigrate to various parts of the world ; they are to be found from South Africa to British Columbia, in the far south of the American continent to the purlieus of Limehouse, but their heart remains in the old home, and however long away they still treasure the recollection of it, and look forward to the day of return.

I have met Chinese in Australia and Northern Canada, on the Witswatersrand of the Transvaal, and divers other places, who, though in some cases more than thirty years had elapsed since they quitted their native land, still awaited the time when they could return and take up their life at the point they had left it a generation before.

A maxim of Chinese social life decrees that all men must marry ; marriage is regarded as a duty, but the preliminaries in connection with it are in direct opposition to those prevailing in the West. It is a commercial transaction ; no love-making marks its inception, no letters protesting undying affection ; the affair is one for adjustment between families and the go-between who is deputed to arrange suitable matches. Once the girl leaves her own home she passes into another world, a new sphere of which she has no previous knowledge, where she may meet a tyrannical mother-in-law, apart from contact for the first time with the man to whom she has been given. He, likewise, has misgivings, since he is uncertain of joy or sorrow, tranquillity or strife, in the future. Most probably an astrologer has been called in to cast the horoscope of the couple, but even then the future is very much on the knees of the gods.

The laws of inheritance are peculiar to the Chinese race. A man is a minor so long as his father is living, and each of the sons inherits in equal portions, the daughters not being taken into account, for they become part of their husband's family. Not only in matters affecting property and inheritance, but in all that pertains to the family circle, the father's authority is the ruling principle, and one that is never questioned. It is, in short, an axiom laid down by Confucius that filial piety and reverence for parents must be consistently practised, and the Chinese people have accepted the dictum as a divine command.

Co-equal with their conception of parental affection is the spiritual force of ancestor worship, whose dominating influence has already been referred to, a widespread form of filial piety that is the basis of Celestial morality.

There are many curious customs linked with ancestor worship ; the spirits passing from this world to the next must be ministered to, their wants supplied, and their descendants are responsible that they do not lack creature comforts. Clothing, food, and money are to be provided for their use. There are striking instances of this, such as a prominent Chinese official who died recently and had his expensive limousine car, equipped with a stuffed chauffeur and footman, duly burnt after his demise, in order that they might be available for him in the next world. This procedure was at variance with the usual custom, since make-believe offerings are the rule and not the exception, and the luxuries offered to the departed take the form of paper models and emblems. For example, money is merely joss-paper with silver painted upon it, these flimsy representations of the genuine article being burnt so that the smoke may carry into the hands of the dead, where they will assume the requisite shape and value.

The future of the living is largely dependent upon the way in which the ritual of ancestor worship is performed. Indeed, the Chinese assert that of all the vital things in life, the most important is to be sure of proper burial.

The foundations of religion in China are laid in this worship, and although it has come into close contact with Western civilisation and the Buddhist faith—both opponents of it—the people remain devotees to the practice, extraneous influences have left this old-world belief untouched, and in the observance of ancestor worship is found the code of morality they observe.

In the urban and agrarian districts the farming and agricultural classes have special relations as between landlord and tenant. As a rule the plots of land are small, for with large families, where the sons share equally with one another, the division of property tends to reduce the individual areas. Where the inheritance is so reduced in size as not to admit of a living being gained, the son may become a tenant farmer, the conditions under which he holds his land being widely different from those in Europe.

Rent obligations are usually met in kind, as obtains in some parts of Italy, the assessment being effected by both landlord and tenant acting in conjunction. In fact, both may attend the cutting of the corn or the rice, supervise the weighing, and then divide the proceeds, the system obviating disputes, whilst arrears of rent need never enter into the bargain.

The system works well in a country of such extent as China, with an illiterate and conservative people, whilst it preserves a cordial atmosphere between landlord and tenant, who are in partnership on mutually advantageous terms. Moreover, class differences and disputes are rare. The landlord takes the rough with the smooth, shares with the lessee whatever he has garnered, and so peace and tranquillity reign, without the next quarter-day hanging like the sword of Damocles over the head of the farmer when the year has been an unprofitable one.

Laws governing agrarian rights are not needed, nor do they exist on the Chinese Statute Book, for both owner and tenant are linked by common ties not calling for any form of legislation.

With regard to Chinese home life, there are many rules bearing on the life of the people, which must, in common with other traits in the national character, be borne in mind in any summing up of the people as a whole.

These I propose to pass in brief review, in the course of which we shall see that there is a distinctly attractive side to the Chinese character, which is revealed in several ways, but none more so than in that of hospitality. A

Chinese dinner has been so often described that there is little about it that is not already known. When given by one of the old conservative type it is a repast without knives or forks, bread or butter, and a tablecloth does not cover the festive board. The dishes are distinctly varied, the ingredients at times of doubtful origin, but the actual cooking has been reduced to a fine art.

Each of the guests is furnished with chopsticks, a spoon, a small wine-cup, and a couple of saucers for condiments and sauces. The table is narrow and polished, and in the centre are dishes containing *hors d'œuvres*. The dinner is preceded by such minor courses as roast melon seeds, nuts, candy, and dessert, after which the main part of the feast commences. The dishes are of an infinite variety, and comprise stag's tendons, bamboo shoots and bamboo roots, pigeon's eggs preserved in chalk—the older the egg, the greater its edible value— lotus seeds, liver of all kinds, sea slugs from the waters around Northern Japan and Vladivostok, and other unique courses. Each dish is served in small bowls, and the acme of politeness is for the host and others to single out dainty morsels on their own plates and deposit them on that of the principal guest. This occasionally has its embarrassing side ; when dining with a war lord once I was not only bombarded with tit-bits from bald and tooth-less old men, opium-sudden magistrates, and convivial warriors, but the host, in addition to contributing from his own plate, toured the table to poach from others for my benefit. At this particular banquet the war lord pro-duced wine of his own concoction, the ingredients being taken from seventy-four different herbs. To preserve inviolate the atmosphere of cordiality and brotherhood, I felt bound to partake of the nauseous liquid, meanwhile reflecting on the trials that beset the British representative when in the performance of his duties.

It is said that there is nothing new under the sun, but one can attend dinners in China that have a certain novelty. In the Flowery Kingdom rats are esteemed a delicacy; I was told they restore the hair in cases of baldness, whilst a stewed black cat will ward off a fever. But the *pièce de résistance* at one of these banquets was a number of newly born white mice served alive, to be dipped in treacle and swallowed like a prairie oyster.

Part of the antipathy aroused in China is due to lack of acquaintance with the lines of thought, etiquette, and peculiar customs, the non-observance of which stirs up Chinese prejudice.

Confucius said that, if you visit a foreign country, first ascertain what is prohibited there, and make yourself *au courant* of the manners and customs of the people you are amongst. This is sound advice, and applies with special force to China. Confucius had a deep and abiding faith in ceremonial and the Chinese, who can be the most polite and courteous people on earth when they like, are strict in its observance.

The observance of ceremonial is much in evidence amongst the governing classes, and merits narration in detail.

The official residence of the district magistrate, or others of the Governmental body, is known as the Yamen, and, like the houses of the Greeks and Romans, single storied and constructed round courtyards open to the skies. The entrance to these inner courtyards is by a large gateway painted in red, the colour symbolical of joy. The gates are of a pattern peculiar to themselves, fold together, and with the handle on the inner side. Passing through this main gateway, you come to others at intervals of ten or a dozen yards, according to the size and importance of the Yamen. They are slightly raised above the ground level, on a small stage or platform with an altar at one side, each doorway leading to a separate courtyard, from which radiate other and smaller ones with quaint moon-shaped arches. The distribution of the personnel of a Yamen is dealt with in the usual practical way. The quarters adjacent to the first gateway are occupied by the doorkeepers and general servants, the offices and guest-rooms are within the first or second courtyard, then farther back come the private apartments and those assigned to the feminine part of the household.

With regard to the gates, there are important rules observed in China ; the number to be opened depends upon the rank and status of the visitor, and they are really the outward and visible sign of his standing. For the ordinary caller the first one only is opened, the remainder being passed by an opening at the side. To the casual visitor it is no easy matter to gain admittance ; in my own case, as a foreign representative, no difficulties were ever presented, and the full number always opened. It is customary to fire a salute on arrival and departure of any visitor of rank, but this is going out under the modern régime, the old-time ritual being shorn of much of its erstwhile picturesqueness.

On arrival the guest is received by the host, who ushers him into the reception hall, taking care to see that he is slightly in advance, whilst with the ultra-courteous Chinese the act of taking seats is simultaneous, so that neither is standing whilst the other is seated. The ceremonial tea is then served, in connection with which there are still more customs to observe. The cup, which has the saucer above instead of below, as with us, is handed to the visitor, who should receive it with both hands. The uninitiated will probably sip the tea forthwith, but this should never be done, as it is the signal for departure, and there is then considerable commotion as attendants and guards take post, and preparations are made to escort the visitor out. It all fits in with the indirect method of doing things in the East ; the host will sip his tea and thus give the requisite hint that he wishes to terminate the visit, having assignations elsewhere.

The failure to observe many of these simple rules of etiquette often leads to difficulties and engenders in the mind of the Celestial, especially of the conservative type, that we are overbearing and ignorant. In a land where such matters are of prime importance it is well to note the laws as expounded by the Chinese. For instance, when passing through a town the first duty is to send one's card to the local official, who may adopt one of several lines of action. He may, in sending his own card, wish you a pleasant journey, which, being interpreted, means that he deems a visit from either side unnecessary. On the other hand, he may call, or send an invitation to dine with him, in which case courtesy demands that the call be returned, and, in any case, a dinner with an educated Chinese adds to knowledge and experience.

The Chinese have a decided sense of humour ; I believe it was a Celestial scribe who declared that humour goes hand in hand with travel, although on occasions it may be grim—especially amongst Orientals.

When acting as the British representative in Chinese Central Asia a short time since, I had occasion to visit a governor who, in accordance with custom, received me on the outskirts of his capital, and personally conducted me to the place prepared for my accommodation. Carriages are limited in Western China, but the governor had produced a Russian landau drawn by three horses abreast, a wheezing vehicle that had probably begun life at a respectable livery stables in Petrograd. Into this state coach we climbed, and proceeded at a hand-gallop to the palace, through streets lined with troops and police. Suddenly without warning our equipage parted in twain, and I found myself, after turning a complete somersault, sitting on the recumbent governor, while the front portion of the carriage, with its two wheels and the driver, was carrying on down the street. My host was greatly upset at this ignoble entry, but he soon saw the humour of it and enjoyed the joke.

A few days later I dined in state with the commander-in-chief, who was not on good terms with the governor, and when I related the incident, and explained that unfortunately I had landed on top of his colleague, he remarked : '' And quite the right place for Your Honour to occupy.''

On another occasion a military officer of high rank

a

14,500 MILES TO LONDON BRIDGE

A milestone in South-West China. They are over 60 feet high, and are placed at intervals of 2½ miles.

THE TOP OF THE WALL OF A CHINESE CITY ON WHICH IT IS POSSIBLE TO DRIVE TWO CARRIAGES ABREAST

Also shows the quaint Chinese corner towers.

dined with me one night, and on taking his place at table gave his richly bedecked and jewelled hat to an attendant. The man was encumbered with a carbine and sword, so cast around for a peg on which to hang his master's headgear, but not perceiving anything suitable, promptly put it on his own head, and there it remained until the war lord left.

On yet another occasion, when I was visiting a famous "tuchun," or military official, who had ambitions towards the presidency and was virtually king over a portion of the Chinese dominions, my host inquired about my domestic existence, when I had arrived in the world, and sundry details as to my present circumstances, adding with some significance that I must certainly be married. On my denying the soft impeachment, he asked if I had no children, and on my regretting that here again I was a defaulter, he said : ''Then what in the world have you been doing all this time?''

Chinese mentality is always amusing, and not infrequently of value, although at times it may be a little disconcerting with its intimate and detailed questions as to one's family life and history. This inclination is common to every Oriental, for he wants to know all about the person he is to meet, and exhibits no reserve in probing matters of intimacy, which, in the West, are considered to mark only the closest stage of friendship. But despite their interrogations the Chinese never lack a sense of humour.

With regard to the lighter side of life, the Chinese are fond of theatricals ; indeed, they may be characterised as the national pastime. The plays are mainly historical and deal with the works and sayings of the sages who quitted this life two to four thousand years ago. There is great reverence for these historical pieces, for they revive the past, and whatever has the stamp of age is accorded first claim to consideration.

The scenery is of a rough and ready kind, and much of it is left to the imagination. There are, of course, regular theatres, as with us, in the larger towns and cities, but in the villages and throughout the vast area of China that really constitutes the nation and will form the public opinion, when this develops, the theatre is a movable affair, and not infrequently set up in a temple courtyard ; if that be not available, then the street is appropriated.

There are no dressing-rooms for actors or actresses, all changes of costume, the arranging and plaiting of the hair, and the painting and powdering of the complexion being carried out in the open, in full view of the crowd, who treat everything as a matter of course. Where the street is chosen as the site, the company takes that part offering the largest area, and they proceed to set up the stage. Meanwhile the street is littered with beams and posts, pedestrians trip up over coils of rope, all traffic is brought to a standstill, or diverted down side streets and alley-ways, until the performance is concluded and the highway once more available to the public.

Foot passengers wishing to gain the far end of the street can do so only by climbing under the stage, bumping their heads at intervals. Yet, despite this appropriation of the main street, an air of cheerfulness prevails, and no resentment is shown by those who are inconvenienced.

There is music in connection with the performance, of a harsh and discordant nature. Confucius was a stanch supporter of musical charm, declaring that through it the moral nature could be reformed. Since that day stagnation has set in, and Chinese music does not produce the effects that it may have done in Confucian days.

Before leaving the social aspect I will deal with an important element in Chinese life that has a direct bearing on the present crisis. This is the organisation and development of trade unions and guilds, and their influence on the well-being of the people.

Trade unionism has existed in China almost since the dawn of history, and for the safeguarding of economic interests the people have long been formed into guilds. These guilds are representative of each trade or profession, with a governing body—analogous to our Chamber of Commerce—to co-ordinate work in the particular city or town. They wield considerable power, the Government of the country takes note of their demands and decisions, and their influence is apparent at every turn. Generally speaking, throughout the twenty-two provinces it is these guilds that determine the taxes and impositions. In the present chaotic state of affairs they play a part, although from their point of view an unsatisfactory one, since in assessments they are at the mercy of the war lords, who back their demands with threats of looting and reprisals against the trader and merchant class, should their requirements not be met.

The limitations of the guild are not confined to mere assessory work ; they act in matters affecting debt and credit between parties, adjust commercial differences that may arise and threaten bankruptcy or financial embarrassment, so that their functions are really a combination of the judicial and mediatory. The guilds are, of course, representative of both the employer of labour and those employed, and such is the bond of union between labour and capital that there is little friction as known in Europe.

In cases where the interests of the workers are concerned or in any way jeopardised, the effect of the guild is felt in the action taken. In Canton, for example, the population is literally a floating one. Upwards of three-quarters of a million spend their lives in sampans, or boats; they are born on the water and end their days beneath the rough thatched roof of a junk, and tread dry land only for supplies and to sell their catches of fish. The boatmen live in close co-operation; in the event of any injustice, real or fancied, they combine, and the whole normal life of the city, in so far as boats and fishing are concerned, is thrown out of gear. Other trades are similarly fortified; they are allied to secure their ends, but the dispute does not usually assume serious form, from the rooted objection to disorder and the love of mediation. Powerful though this combination of trades is, it lacks the sheet anchor of protracted resistance—permanent funds on which to draw to support a prolonged struggle—a drawback that militates against any attempt to force an issue, or to wear down the opposing side. Chinese methods of finance, and the corruption where allotment and distribution of money are concerned, must undergo drastic revision before the effect of a strike can be exerted. Apart from that, so ingrained is the system of peculation and embezzlement that there is always strong mutual suspicion, and a total want of confidence in the integrity of those controlling the funds. Subscriptions towards any strike fund are therefore limited, and this obviates any protracted resistance in the event of a strike.

Trade unions modelled on Western lines are in the making, which means a recasting of the old order of things, and introduction of innovations. This is no light task with ninety-seven per cent. of the people illiterate and essentially creatures of habit, who desire to follow the mode of life pursued by their forefathers, and live in exactly the same way as they did. They are therefore unable to appreciate the points at issue, and, however ably and concisely enunciated, they fail to see anything but a flagrant attempt on ancient custom and an attack on their rights, possibly even to deprive them of their daily bread.

The trade union, as exemplified in China, embraces membership of both master and man ; non-unionists are not admitted to the trade, and members are on a footing of equality. The headquarters of a guild are often equipped as a temple and dedicated to a specific god, or the patron saint of the trade concerned.

The clannish spirit is in constant evidence ; workmen will not allow one from elsewhere to take employment in the district until he has joined the union ; they rarely supplant one another, but a man can make his own terms with the employer, provided he adheres to the minimum wage laid down.

In addition to the trade unions and the guilds, there are clubs distributed throughout the country with the object of providing a meeting-place for those who are provincial residents, and to act as general agents. They organise theatricals and processions, arrange for the burial of deceased members, or despatch of the coffins to their homes. Like the guild-hall, the club-house is often a temple, and dedicated to one of the gods of the three faiths.

The guild and club system does not end here, for there is another associated with families, more particularly the rural districts, and where the settlement is largely composed of a single clan. These are loyal to their own people, they minister to their wants in cases of poverty, and in event of temporary misfortune they are the mainstay of the clan. This explains the cohesion existing amongst the rural masses and the absence of any marked poverty and distress.

The establishment of class and community interests on a definite basis is everywhere apparent. As the administration does not provide for the poor and indigent, they are left to their own resources. So the beggars and mendicant fraternity have their guild, and the Chinese, where the beggars are likely to become a nuisance, or threaten the peace of the neighbourhood, appoint a headman, who is responsible for their good behaviour. These beggar guilds levy contributions on house and shop, thus saving householder and trader. from being importuned. Should there be any refusal to pay the amount in question, the beggars soon bring the refractory one to a sense of his obligations. A dirty and dishevelled party will appear and demand alms. Their presence scares away customers, potential buyers cannot get anywhere near the shop, even if they wish to do so, whilst traffic is held up and all business at a standstill. If the shop-keeper still proves obdurate, his attitude is countered by the arrival of reinforcements, who press their demands for charity until nothing can be heard above the din. Finally, capitulation is forced upon the recalcitrant, and the beggars retire with flying colours.

Closely allied to the guilds and unions are the secret societies, which are honeycombed all over China. Much inaccurate information has been imparted regarding these societies, for when little is known it is easier to imagine. There have been many secret organisations, some of them semi-political and others quasi-religious in form. Generally the object in view has aimed at redress for some injustice on the part of the authorities, but no secret society has ever exerted any influence on the empire as a whole. They possess badges and are divided into grades, with certain forms of initiation into the particular order, and occasionally the rules are such as to introduce an element of force and terrorism, the most recent example of this being a society formed at Chefoo for the studied purpose of ridding the political stage of undesirable opponents.

The Boxers, in 1900, were also a form of secret society, whilst since the inception of the present crisis a number of terrorist clubs has been formed, mainly amongst students of the fanatical type and others inclined towards terrorism.

Although less than three per cent. of the Chinese

people are concerned with politics—and, until quite recently, political agitation held no place in the Chinese mind, nor have they ever shown marked dissatisfaction with the form of government throughout their history until the opening of the twentieth century—times have changed and the secret societies are playing a part in political unrest. The Boxer, or Sword, Society had for its main object the expulsion of foreigners, towards whom they exhibited intense dislike. As the wave of advanced thought and idea passes over China these political organisations will exert more direct influence, until they blossom forth into definite parties.

Nevertheless, it is unlikely to affect the mass of the Chinese people, who are quiet and industrious and capable of considerable endurance. When given to a sudden impulse, it is the result of a cause originating far back, and one that has been undergoing a slow process of development, until in the fulness of time, and for no ostensible reason, it comes into action carrying all before it.

These outbursts can be dealt with on forcible lines, although it would naturally be more politic to remove or obviate the cause. The one hope of improvement lies in the development of education on sound principles, but by a gradual process of evolution. The depredations of war lords have diverted all available money for the upkeep of schools into other channels, to such an extent that the education of the coming generation is mostly in the care of foreign missions. The Dominican Fathers, for instance, at Peking conduct one of the best schools in China for instruction, both written and oral, in the Chinese language.

The demand for books and knowledge is increasing; it is becoming a reality in educated Chinese circles that the whole world must be studied as to fact and application. The classics and writings of the sages cannot determine modern ideas and problems; it is recognised that their solution necessitates a new type of scholar. None can deny that there is a strong undercurrent of intellectualism amongst the student class, but it is far from affecting the masses, who, as already shown, are not only illiterate, but hampered by the variety of dialects spoken, even in single provinces. As a concrete example there is Kiangsi, where over eighty different dialects are spoken, and villagers of one part are unable to make themselves intelligible to those of another.

The condition of the greater part of China at the present moment is similar to that obtaining in Europe during the Middle Ages, and its social and economic evolution must take at least as long as our own in the past. The obstacles confronting them are much more formidable, whether political, religious, or linguistic, and with all the Chinese capacity for work and application, coupled with the spread of education on a wide scale, it is improbable that they would, within the short space of a few years, be able to effect so complete a transformation as Europe only accomplished after several centuries of steady application.

Let us now look at industrial China and the question of labour and employment.

Modern industrialism is becoming an established order along the fringe created by the coast and the various treaty ports, but it has not yet touched the interior, and there is neither code nor system of inspection nor a Civil Service that can enforce legislation regarding work, hours, factories, and employment generally. The Chinese authorities are never lax in the issue of regulations to deal with any given situation, but between the issue and the enforcement there is the widest possible gap. Then there is the financial side ; funds must be devoted to furnish the administrative machinery necessary to see that the regulations are observed in the spirit as well as in the letter. Bribery and corruption being so widespread in China, regulations are frequently the basis of malfeasance and illegal exactions at the hands of officials from those whom the rules are intended to benefit.

In this question of labour, and especially that of juvenile workers in factories and workshops of the cities and towns, whose lot it is most desirable to ameliorate at the earliest opportunity, there are formidable obstacles to overcome, the origin of which must be sought far back in the mists of antiquity. In the first place, the family system, already reviewed, wields power ; its head insists that all the members shall contribute as far as possible to their own support, and under his ancient mandate he feels entitled to exploit them to the utmost.

Most trades and callings are conducted on family lines, and determined opposition awaits those who would alter the hours of labour or conditions of employment. This family loyalty is the personification of virtue, and everything else must be subordinated to it ; not even public duty can precede it, for loyalty as a national expression is non-existent.

Further, as regards agriculture, this is carried on in

the way and with means in vogue during patriarchal times, and there is strong aversion to scrapping them.

We have seen how conservative and devoted the people are to ancient custom and modes of life, and they would certainly misconstrue any attempt, backed though it be with the best of intentions, to interfere with the even tenor of their ways. Public opinion, even when it does assume practical form, would, at the outset at any rate, be hostile to legislation directed towards the recasting of labour conditions, since it would strike a blow at the fundamental principles of local and family control. To overcome the traditions of the past and introduce legislative measures for the working masses is admittedly desirable, but it will be a question of two or more generations.

The foregoing remarks show that the force of habit is strong in China, where ancient custom reigns supreme, and probably three hundred and ninety millions of the people heed not the passing of empires and the onward march of progress. The instinct to go on in the same old way is inherent, and, although there is improvement, none can say that there has been any definite change in conditions that have prevailed since before the Christian era.

An able Chinese diplomatist, with whom I discussed this question at length, agreed that although for centuries the people had been accustomed to the declarations of imperial policy, and publication of edicts with definite orders as to what they were to do, it is not within the power of any legislative body, however representative, to break through the rules of ancestor worship, to alter

the state of feeling and of thought, or to interfere with
the bonds holding Society together, without full regard
being paid to the mentality of the people. It is possible
of accomplishment given ample time, but the evolution
must be slow and carefully directed, for any check might
bring about a reaction from the innate superstition and
distrust of innovations.

Some examples of prevalent beliefs will illustrate this.
Taking mineral development, the deterrent to opening
up the vast resources of China is traceable to superstition
and prejudice. There is the dragon-winged monster, Feng
Sui, the guardian of hidden treasures, who annihilates
all offending him. A few years ago it was proposed to
develop some of the rich coalfields in Shensi, but the
people deprecated such action, for, they said, the area
in question was the home of the mighty dragon who, if
his slumbers were disturbed, would issue forth and spread
fire, death, and pestilence through the land. So the
dragon slept on, and the coalfields remained untapped.
Then again, in the same province, a drought occurring
in the summer of 1926, the governor, yielding to his
own and the people's settled beliefs, introduced a
memorial tablet reputed to be possessed of miraculous
powers, its worship being enjoined as the concrete means
of terminating the drought.

The Chinese gave us the mariner's compass, and they
have been prominent in astronomy, but where an eclipse
occurs the officials and the people in conjunction amass
every kind of ear-splitting instrument, and by over-
whelming din and noise endeavour to scare away the
demon that is passing.

Where reforms have been introduced in the past they have usually had an ulterior motive ; personal greed and aggrandisement are the main considerations in public service, and the action of the reformers has stultified the movement and increased the popular suspicion.

I have already remarked that not three per cent. of the Chinese nation is in any way concerned with politics. Confucius declared that those who interfere therein are playing a dangerous game, the government should be left to the appointed officials, and that he who does not occupy the post must not interfere with the discharge of its duties and obligations. In the popular estimation government is by divine authority, built up on precedent, communicated to the people through definite channels, and in conformity with the standard of conduct to which they are accustomed. It follows, then, that to introduce a form of self-government that must obviously clash with tradition and legend, to inculcate the principles of a politically minded and self-conscious people, such as we have in Europe, the old order must go. But much remains to be done before that can be accomplished.

It may be argued that the Republic in China has set aside this old order, but from what has been said above it is clear that the transformation is a phantom one. The record of the past fifteen years has killed all faith in the aims and intentions of those struggling on the various sides. The country is split up into small areas controlled by bandit chiefs and military opportunists imbued with personal ambition and greed, let loose upon the district, wherever it may be, and holding the view that they are as fully entitled to power and authority as those in office

at the moment. The central and western provinces—
Szechuan, for example, with a population of seventy
millions—are overrun with these predatory bands ; commandeering of labour by the '' armies '' of these brigands
and war lords is the rule rather than the exception,
those so impressed receiving no pay or consideration at
the hands of the press gangs, beyond possibly a certifi-
cate exempting them from further service with the forces,
but as the next arrival is almost certain to be an opponent
of he who has gone before, the paper given to the
labourer is valueless.

To such an extent has the reign of terror gone through
the country, and reduced almost to vanishing-point the
possibilities of establishing a constitutional and representative government in the interests of the people, that
there are districts as large as Lancashire presided over
by chieftains who rule with a rod of iron, scorning
interference with their rights and prerogatives. They are
in so strong a position that the central authority, when
it exists, prefers to treat with them on a delicate basis,
rather than run the inevitable risk of creating an enemy
whom it is impossible to reach without the aid of a paid
army, organised on modern and disciplined lines, and
capable of undertaking a campaign beset with physical
and other difficulties.

The obstacles in the way of introducing change, and
effecting improvements, will be plain to the reader, and
in a subsequent chapter I shall endeavour to show, from
a careful analysis of past and present events, what the
future may contain for the economic and political
evolution of China.

ARMY AND POLICE

CHAPTER III

ARMY AND POLICE

IT is only within recent years that the Chinese military system has undergone revision, mainly at the hands of Japanese instructors, who in the west and in the interior, especially that part of the Celestial dominions adjacent to Russia, brought into being the New Model troops. These were, for a time, in a fair state of efficiency, but have since degenerated in common with other forces in the Republic.

The principal result of the Chino-Japanese War of 1894-95 revealed the lamentable state of Chinese forces, naval and military, and need for drastic reform if China wished to assert her authority. Prior to that event the national defences take us back to the days before the standing armies of Europe; military science was still in a most primitive state, and the means to combat opponents were such as courted defeat at the hands of any modern adversary. The ancient classics were the guide to strategy and tactics, as well as in the general development of character.

The Chinese are remarkable for their tenacity and patience, and nowhere are there finer illustrations of these traits in the national temperament than in the record of their various military operations. One of the most striking was in connection with the Chinese army detailed

63

to quell a revolution in the far west in 1876. The march of this army across China for the recovery of the lost province was entrusted to General Tang, a nondescript force was given him, and with these, and a few general instructions, he set out from Peking for the goal four thousand miles to the west.

As long as they were in a more or less inhabited area the army lived on the country, but once beyond the confines of comparative civilisation this was no longer possible, for supply and transport services did not exist, and the districts traversed were unable to provide the force with the requisite supplies.

General Tang was, however, equal to the occasion. He collected and halted his scattered and roving army, chose the most promising area and there marked out the ground around the camps and bivouacs ; the sword, the gun, and the lance were laid aside, and in their place were taken up the spade and plough. The ground was prepared, cereals and vegetables were sown, and in the fulness of time the crops were garnered, and so, with renewed supplies, the army resumed its march, the goal was reached, and the rebellious province again brought under the imperial sway.

Even as at present constituted the Chinese forces are a collection of units, operating for the personal advancement of its own particular commander, and, as will be seen, the army has no national character, nor is it in any way organised on national lines.

With the advent of the Republic in 1911 the work of reconstructing the army was taken in hand, and a force of 50 divisions, totalling 500,000 men, was agreed upon.

BAMBOO SUSPENSION BRIDGE, SLUNG ON BAMBOO ROPES, AND
ABOUT 700 FEET LONG
It crosses the river just below the dam

HOUSES OUTSIDE CITY WALL, CHUNG-KING
The water rises at flood time and covers a large part of these houses.

This number was considered adequate for defence of the Republic as a whole, and by a Presidential decree of August, 1912, a programme was laid down for the War Ministry. This was to be preceded by the disbandment of the various forces scattered over the country, where units worked under their own provincial chief, without regard to any national object. These had arisen with the revolution and the chaos resulting from overthrow of the monarchy, and it was resolved to disband them as an essential preliminary to stabilising the Government, but it was not until 1913 that President Yuan Shih Kai had established a hold upon the country. There was demoralisation throughout the provinces, want of confidence in the Government; the losses inflicted by warring elements, and active propaganda had produced an intense spasm throughout China. Disorder increased, and the efforts to demobilise met with strenuous opposition, for it meant depriving large numbers of men of a livelihood and unlimited scope for loot and personal gain. The tension was accentuated by the treatment meted out to different provinces, varying in its scope and partiality, so that very soon Yuan Shih Kai was compelled to garrison several of them as a precautionary measure.

All China was overrun with predatory bands, mutinies occurred amongst them, some of a dangerous character, and all were affected by the political developments of the time. On one point most were agreed—the overthrow of the Manchu dynasty, and the military leaders who had contributed to that end were acclaimed as heroes, civil offices and power were open to them, and the

5

military caste, which had for centuries been regarded with disdain and as a profession that ranked low in the social order, became predominant, the hold they gained steadily increasing from that moment. The old order of things was reversed, the pendulum swung back, and the *literati* were relegated to the background.

This moment marks an era in Chinese history, for it saw not only the rise of the military party, but creation of the "tuchun" system—that is, the appointment of military governors above the civil provincial chiefs—a drastic step destined to have disastrous consequences. From it resulted decentralisation of military authority, an almost immediate fall in the morale of the forces, and a total want of uniformity in arms, equipment, general training, and efficiency.

A new figure had appeared, and the direction of affairs in the twenty-two provinces passed to other hands. Meanwhile the authority of the Central Government was being undermined through intrigue, endless plots, and internecine warfare, the power and greed of the tuchuns grew in proportion, and they found a sure and swift method of aggrandisement.

Gradually the factor of self-interest became all-absorbing ; each looked upon his own particular province as a domain over which he could exercise absolute control, wherein he could levy such taxes and imposts as would yield the maximum revenue short of goading the people to desperation, and where he might entrench and fortify his position with a view to attacking other tuchuns, and to wage war upon his neighbour as the feudal barons did in our own history.

Immense sums were allocated by the Central Government for the upkeep of those provincial armies who were more or less loyal to it. Some of them, especially in provinces remote from Peking, drew funds from the central Treasury for the maintenance of forces that existed mainly on paper. The returns sent in to the War Ministry indicated considerable forces at salient points, but the true relation between the actual and paper strength of a Chinese unit is so indeterminate that it would be impossible to form any reliable estimate even with those returns available. Peculation and embezzlement reigned supreme. Perhaps the most glaring example of this was seen in the largest of the western provinces, where I witnessed an inspection of the forces carried out by a general officer deputed from the War Ministry.

The arrival of this inspector from the central seat of government warned the tuchun that his bogus army would be exposed to the glaring light of day, but, being a man of resource, and knowing that an inspecting officer can be induced to imitate Nelson and his famous "blind eye," if sufficient inducement be forthcoming, he despatched press gangs to all the provincial towns and villages, commandeering every male subject from fifteen to upwards of fifty years of age, so that the total might, at any rate, bear some relation to the paper figure. The supply of uniform was a simple matter, for it consisted merely of jacket and trousers, a stock of all necessary articles being held in readiness in the provincial arsenals and stores against any such eventuality as the present. The inspection duly took place, the general departed, and matters resumed the even tenor of their ways.

Expansion gave place to shrinkage, the vast sums that had been earmarked for this province in the past were automatically renewed, and continued to be paid until the final collapse of any central authority.

History has no parallel to the state of affairs prevalent throughout China to-day amongst the military factions. The soldiers move from one army to another ; the defeat of one tuchun by a rival jeopardises their pay and position, so they pass on to another army, espouse its cause and promote its fortunes, so long as their pay and existence are guaranteed. As an alternative they may join the various roving bands infesting the country ; they can, and do, prey upon the people, and thrive by robbery and violence.

The area of some provinces being equal to England and Wales demands division into sections presided over by subordinates of the military governor, who, in their turn, when feeling secure in their section, set up in opposition to their superior, or join hands with another who may hold out sufficient inducement. Thus the higher command has to maintain a hawk-like watch over its subordinates, and the menace of disruption and conspiracy is constant. To break up these numerous semi-independent States and armed formations will be the task of those who essay the unification of China—an immense undertaking in a country of such extent, so varied and illiterate in the number of its people, and so devoid of suitable roads and means of communication for the successful prosecution of military operations to that end.

Such standardisation as exists in the Chinese army

to-day is mostly centred on personal grounds. Each unit of a command is known by the name of its commanding officer, and the organisation most generally adopted is that of the division and brigade. Generally speaking, a division comprises two brigades, each of two regiments of infantry, a regiment of cavalry, and a number of field batteries, varying with the total available. In addition, there are engineer units, transport, and machine-gun sections. With the more highly organised, military police and an indifferent field hospital are included, the total strength on paper of the division being approximately 11,000. No reliance can, however, be placed on this figure, since it varies with the commander and is subject to circumstances peculiar to Chinese military procedure.

The badges of rank and type of uniform are on the Japanese model, and in the training and equipment the influence of the latter is in constant evidence.

Uniformity in detail does not exist, and although the Japanese and Russian system of distinction between units and grades has been adopted, the badges being worn on arm or collar as the case may be, some of the provinces, notably in the west and south-west, bear the insignia of rank or unit on the front and back of the tunic or jacket, as was formerly the accepted idea in the Chinese army.

Arms and equipment are principally on the Japanese or German model, but the Chinese arsenals have also produced a weapon which is a combination of both but inferior to either. More than seventy per cent. of the rifles, revolvers, and machine-guns are in a state of neglect, with no proper arrangement for their overhaul and repair.

The Chinese, with their usual perspicacity, saw the value of machine-guns in the European war, and nearly every division has its complement, those of Japanese make being in the majority, although, as in the case of rifles, machine-guns are manufactured in some of the arsenals from an assortment of European patterns.

Scattered over China are arsenals conducted on European or Japanese lines ; they number eighteen, of which only five are at the moment nominally subject to Peking, or the Northern force. In addition to this total there are innumerable workshops and petty arsenals, some capable of producing crude powder and shot and undertaking repair work of a simple nature. The output of these arsenals is controlled by the tuchun of the province, and it not infrequently happens that arms and equipment manufactured are sold by the officer in charge to another chief or independent war lord in adjacent territory.

With the Northern and Southern forces there are administrative, supply, and transport services of a rough and ready nature, but, like the Chinese theatre and its scenery, much is left to the imagination. For example, the medical service is of a sketchy character, even amongst the Russian-organised units of the Cantonese forces. In 1912, concurrently with general reform, provision was made for the establishment of an army medical department, and a medical college was set up in Peking in that year. Given time and opportunity, it might have developed into a useful service, but it has perished in the general chaos. The care of the wounded, as well as medical and sanitary measures generally, is looked upon as outside the scope of an army ; surgery is non-existent, and such arrangements as exist in both contending forces are mostly in the hands of foreign missions, or voluntary workers of that nature, who minister on a limited scale to the wants of sick and wounded. The mortality resulting from lack of medical attention is necessarily heavy ; men wounded in the fighting-line receive only the crudest treatment, and in the event of serious wounds little can be done for them.

In many cases the wounded are not even removed from the battlefield ; they must lie where they fall, or they may be fortunate in being carried to a rough shelter and deposited on the bare ground, to recover or die. In other words, it is a survival of the fittest.

To a large extent the Chinese army lives upon the country and draws its sustenance as it goes. Moreover, the needs of the Celestial soldier are far easier to meet than in the case of his European or American prototype, so the commissariat can be left largely to the soldiers themselves.

Coolie labour is the main element in transport, carts being used where practicable, but improvisation of the usual makeshift character is the rule.

It is obvious that military reform cannot be effected without foreign assistance, which the Chinese are now more than ever chary of employing, from the dread of admitting the influence which they regard as contributing to the present status and the undermining of their sovereign rights. A complete series of officers from the highest ranks downwards is necessary, trained to regard war as a science ; supply and transport, medical, pay, clothing, and other administrative departments must be created, together with formation of a competent staff.

Military education in China is likewise in a state of disorganisation ; the best school is that now presided over by the Bolshevik Military Committee at Canton, a cadet college that has upwards of 3,000 pupils, from whose ranks the commissioned grades of the Cantonese army have been mainly supplied, and to it may be ascribed much of the success hitherto achieved by the Southern operations.

The visit to this country in 1926 of a mission composed of Chinese military officers, presided over by General Hsu, who was recently assassinated, was to a considerable extent concerned with aviation and the possibility of extending the new arm and latest mode of transport in the Chinese Republic. A commercial aviation service had been established under British and foreign auspices in 1919 with a British officer as supervisor, and about 140 aeroplanes were purchased. The scheme went well for a time ; the Chinese novice proved himself an apt pupil in the study of aeronautics and the art of flying, but the schemes propounded for development of commercial air lines terminated in failure, the machines purchased becoming the prey of sundry war lords and the principal opposing sides.

The pay of the various ranks of the Chinese army is laid down on a scale that is only partially adhered to. It varies from four taels for a private to six hundred per month for a general officer, but in so far as the simple soldier is concerned the amount ostensibly due to him has to filter through many channels and only reaches him in an attenuated form. What actually happens in more than half the provinces is that the soldiers are expected to make their own arrangements with regard to money and subsistence ; illegal taxation and forced contributions are countenanced, and no check is given to their demands upon the people.

The illicit methods of supplying the wants of provincial armies is probably not realised in Europe and America, notably the exploitation of opium.

The opium question has always been a vital one with China. The efforts made to eradicate the evil were bearing good fruit, and by 1917 she was comparatively free from the blight. The new state of affairs was short-lived. Many of the provinces were already quasi-independent ; funds from a central source not being forthcoming, ways and means had to be devised to meet the deficiency. The war lords and independent bandit chiefs were quick to see a profitable source of income in the cultivation of the poppy, by which they could pay and support their troops, and so the traffic in opium again flourishes unchecked and in a new rôle.

Having dealt with the military forces as a whole, I leave a discussion of the strength and composition of the Northern and Southern armies to a later chapter.

It is appropriate to give an account here of civil protection and police organisation, in order to complete the survey of the military and civil defence systems.

A Presidential decree of 1914 indicated the lines to be followed in police organisation, this being based on the old system, under which the district magistrate was the chief police officer of his area. The latter is a versatile official ; the title represents but inadequately his numerous functions, which are educational, judicial, fiscal, and all that pertains to an executive. We have seen that he is the one official who comes into direct contact with the people and is responsible for law and order, in normal times at any rate.

Despite the prevalent chaos, the system of administration continues in much the same way as it has always done. As a general rule the city and town is divided into quarters, subdivided into wards, each under a minor official corresponding to a police inspector with us. In the western provinces some of the towns are surrounded by a wall, with gateways in conformity with the points of the compass.

Under the police inspector are watchmen, who perambulate the streets at night. None of these individuals is paid by the State, but they are authorised to collect a small fixed sum weekly from every householder and shopkeeper in their ward. All those who come in from outlying districts for the weekly market-day are liable to this imposition, and no exception is taken to the procedure.

A ward numbers from eighty to one hundred houses, and has a watchman allotted to it, and whenever there is a sale of property within its limits the watchman is entitled to a commission. Should there be any default in payment, or the sums due be in arrears, the police and watchmen have their own methods for bringing the delinquent to book. They either ignore the house or shop, as the case may be, or, in extreme circumstances, when this fails, achieve the desired result by the simple arrangement of a burglary.

It will be seen that the police and watchmen are paid. by the public, but they are also recompensed by the thieves and gambling community, so that we have the phenomenon of the two powers of light and darkness in league against the public. It not infrequently happens that the police are themselves the receivers of stolen goods and play a leading part in the division of the spoils.

Despite the Chinese assurances given to Great Britain, the United States, and Japan in 1902 that drastic improvements would be instituted in conduct and management of prisons, a revision of the Chinese code of law, and complete rearrangement of judicial and criminal procedure, in order to bring it into line with that of Western nations and so justify us in handing over our respective subjects to the tender mercies of Chinese law, the improvements effected in the period of twenty years agreed upon are negligible. Indeed, in 1922 it was only confusion worse confounded, for in the meantime the Republic had been set up, anarchy and chaos reigned supreme, and the lot of prisoners throughout China was a sorry one. True, there is the "model" prison in Peking, constructed in 1912 on the American system, and an example of what a prison should be, but it is by no means a fair representation of the provincial gaol.

Russia voluntarily relinquished her extra-territorial rights, whilst those of Germany and Austria were, *ipso facto,* cancelled by the war. Europeans of those nationalities can, therefore, be seen with Chinese in the prison in question, but unfortunately it stands out in solitary glory, and gives the case of prison affairs and conduct elsewhere in China a false aspect.

Up to the spring of 1926 the routine in the "model" gaol at Peking compared favourably with that of Europe and America ; there were regular meals, in the proportion of two for a Chinese and three for a European prisoner, with baths at regular intervals, and a working day of approximately nine hours. Various trades are taught, or, at any rate, work of sorts is carried out in them, and the prisoners are kept occupied and so prevented from degenerating through prolonged inactivity and lack of moral and physical recreation. In the case of those sentenced to solitary confinement, three days is the maximum period at one time, the cells being eight to nine feet square.

With that rapidity which characterises the Orient when European supervision is withdrawn, this "model" prison, since the climax of April, 1926, when the President fled from the capital and government disappeared, has fallen from its high estate. Yet it is only another example of the indifference and decay that assert themselves when the guiding hand of order and progress is no longer at the helm.

Since the earliest days of her history China has had a Department of Justice, but only in 1912 was it separated from the executive and formed as a distinct body. So loose, however, is the organisation and control that the judiciary has no power, and cases are rarely referred to it. Such questions as may arise in a province,

PEKING
The marble boat and bridge on the Lotus Lake of the Summer Palace.

PEKING
The main street and Beggar's Bridge viewed from the City Wall.

and should be adjudicated by the supreme court, are not always so dealt with, but if the necessity arises they are referred to the Ministry of the Interior.

A high court has been set up in some of the provinces, which decides important civil and criminal cases and also appeals from local metropolitan courts.

The spirit and conduct of the old régime are reflected in the legal procedure at the present time. In spite of the provisions of the criminal code, that lay down with Chinese thoroughness on paper that which is rarely, if ever, followed in practice, the magistrates do not study diligently or "make themselves perfect in the know-ledge of the laws," nor are they assisted by subordinates with claim to legal qualification. Indeed, the latter are merely clerks, who prepare the written statements and take down evidence, as well as attending to memoranda for both accused and defendant. With such an irregular procedure, unqualified judges, and lack of probity, it is not surprising that the road to justice is devious and beset with numerous difficulties.

It is, of course, recognised that China is in a state of disorganisation, and that time is needed to reform the judicial procedure, but although it is several years since the laws were more or less recodified, they have not been applied with sincerity, and in the existing chaos and ever-increasing anarchy there is but slight possibility of their being satisfactorily administered in the near future.

With the establishment of the Republic in 1911 the Japanese code was imposed practically as it stood, being revised to suit the needs and customs of the Chinese.

For the reasons already indicated, this reform has also been shelved—temporarily, at any rate.

In criminal cases the Chinese courts move slowly, obstacles are cast in the path of justice, and the flimsiest excuses are given for non-fulfilment of ordinary legal forms. The law of Habeas Corpus is unknown, and a person may be in gaol indefinitely awaiting trial. Indeed, it would not be going too far to say that with the frequent change of officials a man might be there for so long that no record of his offence can be traced; the why and the wherefore have been forgotten; only the man himself is extant, still undergoing the punishment of his lost crime.

I have remarked on the condition of Chinese prisons. There realism can be studied with effect; little tendence is given the prisoners, and often food must be found by friends or relatives. The date of trial in the courts is vague, an appeal is of little avail, whilst justice and mercy may alike be denied, as was recently the case with an unfortunate official who was arrested and shot without trial by a leading tuchun on what was known to be a false charge.

Moreover, evidence in the police and local courts, if they may be so styled, rarely holds good against counter-evidence offered by a Chinese subject. Whatever the rights of a foreign national might be, in a matter concerning land, for instance, the magisterial decision is usually in favour of the Chinese subject.

FOREIGN RELATIONS AND INFLUENCE

CHAPTER IV

FOREIGN RELATIONS AND INFLUENCE

So much of the propaganda disseminated in the past two years by Cantonese Government agents, and their Russian advisers, has been devoted to discrediting all treaties and trade with foreigners that the general reader doubtless imagines the Kuomintang leaders to be more concerned with the expulsion of foreigners than with the defeat of the North. The truth is, of course, that the Southern Government, influenced by Soviet Russia, anxious to destroy European and American influence in the Far East, has raised the anti-foreign cry as a means to gain the popularity of the masses, and thus facilitate the task of conquering the still formidable opposition centred on Peking.

"Drive out the foreigners who are battening upon poor China," shout the Moscow-inspired propagandists of Canton, "and China will at last be rich, powerful, and free." It is a catch-phrase that has often figured in Chinese history. From the earliest times trade with China has been confronted with opposition and difficulties found in no other country. The widespread belief that foreigners were exploiting a defenceless China was partly responsible for the Boxer rising, and it has been the trumpet-call of most aspirants for power during the past twenty-five years.

To-day, while the Central Government is opposed to measures of violence against foreigners, both North and South demand the cancellation of privileges at present enjoyed by other nations in China.

Is that demand justified ? Let us examine the facts and trace the course of events from the day when the first British ship, feeling its way through the dangers of an unknown Pacific Ocean by the aid of a chart found in a captured Spanish vessel, crept up the river to Canton, the oldest port in the East, and there endeavoured to open trade with the Viceroy of the Ming Emperor.

This pioneer British ship reached Canton in A.D. 1637, but owing to the opposition of the authorities, encouraged, it is believed, by Portuguese and Spanish seamen who had preceded it, no trade resulted, and the vessel was forced to return.

More ships attempted to secure cargoes of tea, silks, spices, and other articles for which China was already becoming famous, but little progress was made until A.D. 1685, when, about forty years after the Manchu dynasty had consolidated its hold on China, an imperial decree was issued cancelling the regulations under which foreign ships could trade only at Canton, and declaring all ports open to foreign vessels.

The way now seemed clear for the speedy development of a trade which would be lucrative to both nations. So it was thought by the East India Company, the merchant pioneers who at that time ruled India under a Charter from the British Crown. This company despatched their first trading vessel to Canton, opening a warehouse there in order to increase the volume of goods that could be shipped to Europe.

At this juncture one of those sudden changes of policy ensued which have frequently figured in the history of foreign relations with China. The Emperor died, his successor promptly reversing the previous liberal policy, and closing all Chinese ports to foreign ships with the single exception of Canton. Moreover, a number of annoying restrictions was imposed upon traders by the new Emperor, who regarded himself as supreme ruler over all the earth, and Europeans as barbarians whose influence, if allowed to grow, might in time conflict with his own authority.

These restrictions increased in severity until, in 1757, trade between foreign nations and China was limited to Canton, and placed under the direction of the Co-Hong, a group of thirteen merchants who, by imperial decree, were appointed "Emperor's Merchants" and given a monopoly of all trade.

They were controlled in their business dealings by an official collector appointed by the Emperor, whose duty it was to ensure that the special requirements of the throne were complied with. Under this arrangement, which existed from 1757 to 1842, foreign ships were permitted to visit Canton for commercial purposes during the trading season, providing they paid the high duties demanded by the Canton collector.

On its conclusion everyone was directed to quit, no foreigner of any nation being permitted to remain on Chinese soil when not actually trading from his ship.

With commerce thus hampered, it says much for the

tenacity of the early seamen that any trade at all was done. Nevertheless, between 1793 and 1810 the value of tea exported from China was £27,000,000, the sale price in England amounting to £55,000,000, a profit of over 100 per cent. The value of opium imported into China by British traders during the period 1790 to 1840 was upwards of 500,000 chests, with a gross value of £100,000,000.

With the advantages of increased commerce and the growing demand from Europe for articles from China, it is only natural that the drastic restrictions imposed by the Manchu Emperor should cause considerable dissatisfaction.

The prevailing discontent among British merchants, who had now almost monopolised the trade between China and the outside world, resulted in the British Government of the day despatching to Peking in 1792 the first official mission to China, in charge of Lord Macartney.

His instructions were to obtain permission from the Emperor for the establishment of a British embassy at Peking, in order that official relations between the two countries might be placed upon a definite footing, and trading difficulties overcome by negotiation on the spot.

At the outset this first attempt to initiate friendly relations was doomed to failure. Upon his arrival Lord Macartney discovered that the Emperor, as the Son of Heaven and supreme ruler over all earthly peoples, expected the representative of the British throne to "kow-tow," or prostrate himself, before the throne as a sign of allegiance. This Lord Macartney declined to do, and for some days there was a deadlock. Eventually the Emperor agreed to waive the kow-tow, but the results of this first meeting between a British diplomat and a Chinese ruler were negative.

Acting on his determination not to permit an increase of foreign influence in China, the Emperor rejected the proposal for an embassy, and also refused to alter in any way the restrictions previously imposed on British trade.

A further effort to improve relations was made in 1816, when Lord Amherst was sent to China, but this attempt likewise failed in its object. The undoubted collapse of these early endeavours to bring China into the comity of nations was due to insistence upon the British missions accepting a basis of inferiority, a demand with which the delegates would not comply. How strenuous were the difficulties encountered in this direction will be realised by the fact that a communication sent by the Chinese Emperor to the King, George III., in the year following the failure of the Macartney mission, ended with the words : "It is that you may long obey that I address you this imperial command."

In 1833 the monopoly hitherto enjoyed by the East India Company of trading with China was abolished, and all British traders were placed on terms of equality in this lucrative and growing branch of our foreign commerce. Yet another attempt to overcome difficulties imposed by China was inaugurated by the appointment of Lord Napier as Britain's representative in China. The aim was to make him our first ambassador to that country, but to overcome Celestial antagonism to the presence of foreign political representatives, Lord Napier was sent as superintendent of trade.

In the China of that day the trader occupied a lowly position in social life, and, largely owing to this fact, our new superintendent was treated with disrespect, for it was beyond Chinese conception to understand how the representative of a king could be engaged in commerce. Lord Napier's task was made more difficult because at this time, apart from the inherent dislike of Chinese officialdom to have dealings with foreign nations, the imports of China exceeded exports, and consequently upset the balance of trade. This, the Chinese authorities feared, would in time cause a money famine in China. The crisis came in 1839, when, thoroughly alarmed by the increase in the quantity of opium imported into China by British traders, as well as by the drain of money required to pay for these imports, the Emperor despatched a special commissioner to Canton with instructions to close the opium traffic. In compliance with his mandate, a stock of 20,283 chests of opium, valued at £2,000,000, then in the British warehouses at Canton, was seized. Further, the Emperor's commissioner demanded a bond from British merchants guaranteeing that the trade in opium should cease, coupling with it the condition that sixteen leading foreigners—several of them having no connection with the trade—should be hostages against further importation of the drug by any foreign nation.

The confiscation of this opium, and the demands accompanying it, rendered action by the British Government imperative, and led to what is known as the " Opium War " of 1840.

Since it has been freely stated by Cantonese propagandists that this war was an example of commercial aggression, I would point out—without necessarily being in accord with our action at that period—that prior to this crisis opium had been imported into China overland from India and elsewhere, being welcomed as a preventive of malarial fever. There was an enhanced demand for the Indian article by reason of its superior quality to that grown locally.

The Opium War of 1840 was fought as much to enforce the right of diplomatic intercourse between the two nations on terms of equality as to secure redress for the just grievances of traders. Now that the monopoly of the East India Company had expired, it was felt in England that a position of inferiority, which necessitated Lord Napier addressing any note in " humble " terms to a third-rate subordinate of the imperial Viceroy at Canton, could no longer be tolerated.

Moreover, additional regulations were drafted, still further limiting trade and intercourse with foreigners. Those dealing with the latter had their shops destroyed, factories were blockaded, and foreign merchants held as prisoners—outrages to which we could not submit.

Hostilities were opened by the arrival of a fleet of sixteen warships and a force of 4,000 troops. This combination proceeded to blockade Canton, which was later bombarded and its forts stormed.

The Viceroy then offered a ransom equivalent in value to the opium confiscated, and also agreed to cede Hong

Kong, an island inhabited by a few fishermen, as a place where the British might build up a trading town.

A general settlement was embodied in the Treaty of Nanking of 1842, the first to regularise the conditions of British trade with China, and a document still governing many of the relations between the two countries. By this instrument the five cities of Shanghai, Amoy, Nanking, Foochow, and Canton were declared treaty ports and thrown open to all nations. The monopoly hitherto held by thirteen "Imperial Merchants" at Canton was abolished, Hong Kong was ceded to the British in perpetuity, the imperial tariff was enforced, and foreign officials were accorded equal status with those of China.

One of the signatory powers to the Treaty of Nanking was the United States, who thus extended her influence to the Far East for the first time, and took her place as a factor in world problems there.

For some years after the war there was considerable anti-foreign feeling, especially amongst officials and those around the throne. Engagements were entered into with foreign representatives, and then evaded or disputed. The inability of officials to control the people placed the lives of those seeking trade in the newly opened ports in constant jeopardy. The Chinese, not understanding this contact with Europe after nearly forty centuries of isolation, were openly hostile to the new developments. Only a spark was needed to start a conflagration.

It came with the capture of the Chinese crew of a British ship in 1856. According to the accepted canons of international law, the Chinese were on British territory, and therefore immune from arrest by Chinese officials until extradition proceedings had been taken in British courts. The responsible officials, however, cared little for international law, and their action necessitated an ultimatum, followed by combined British and French action to compel the Chinese to honour their agreements.

With the Franco-British force were diplomatic representatives of Russia and the United States, the latter being evidence that the importance of China was now equally realised in the New World as in the Old.

When the troops were within striking distance of Peking the imperial commissioners surrendered. Of the four treaties signed in 1858, that with Great Britain was the only one conferring upon a foreign Power the right of permanent diplomatic residence in Peking itself.

These treaties were to have been ratified in the following year, but the Chinese, fearful of the growing contact with foreign Powers, once more changed their minds, and when the British, French, and American representatives arrived at Taku they found the river barricaded and the forts fully manned. They were further informed that if desirous of communication with the Emperor they must enter China by a "side door"—at a place called Peitang, higher up the coast.

This studied affront to three Great Powers, although resented by the American Minister, had, perforce, to be accepted by him. It met with determined action by Great Britain and France, and, as no satisfaction was forthcoming, overtures for an amicable adjustment being rejected, a small expeditionary force was despatched. This found itself unable to overcome the Taku forts, and it was only in the following year that a Franco-British army, landing at Peitang, occupied Peking.

Before the arrival of this expedition the Emperor, Hsien Feng, fled to the summer palace at Yuen Ming Yuen, five miles from the city, leaving his brother, Prince Kung, as regent with full powers to negotiate terms. The new treaty between Great Britain and China was signed with full ceremony on October 24, and by its provisions five further ports were opened to world commerce—Tientsin, Chefoo, Newchang, Kiukiang, and Chinkiang. A similar treaty was signed by the French, the end of the campaign being marked by an astute diplomatic move on the part of the Russian representative. On learning that the allied army was shortly to be withdrawn from Peking, he approached Prince Kung, offering to use his influence to secure the removal of the Franco-British troops, provided the regent would cede to Russia the Primorsk province of China. By this move Russia secured valuable territory between the Ussuri River and the sea coast facing Japan, a coastline extending for 700 miles.

For some years following the signing of the Convention of Peking, China was immersed in internal troubles, notably the famous Tai-ping Rebellion, which, beginning in 1853 by the capture of Nanking, lasted ten years and cost 20,000,000 lives.

In 1876 the Chefoo Treaty was signed, which still further regulated trade between Great Britain and China, and laid down conditions governing the opium traffic. It also sanctioned the opening of four new treaty ports and six landing-places on the Yangtse River.

Fourteen Chinese ports were now open to foreign trade. Matters were comparatively quiet until 1897, when what may be characterised as the "Battle of Concessions" ensued. Germany occupied Kiaochao, Russia secured Port Arthur, and Great Britain Weihaiwei, while the French took over Kwang-chow-wan.

Trade was still seriously handicapped, the main difficulty being the refusal of the Chinese authorities, continued with one exception to the present day, to allow foreigners to own land or property in China. This problem, eased for a short time when Hong Kong was developed as a British colony, became acute after the opening of further ports to foreign trade in 1876.

The solution of the difficulty, suggested by the Chinese Government, and accepted by British business interests, was the segregation of foreigners on land set aside for their use and leased to the nation concerned. Thus came into being the British and foreign concessions, which have since, as at Shanghai, grown into flourishing modern cities. In view of Cantonese agitation against the presence of foreigners with special rights on Chinese soil, it should be remembered that the system of building miniature cities, owned, occupied, and municipally administered by the subjects of European nations and the United States, originated with the Chinese themselves.

So far as Great Britain is concerned, we have concessions at Amoy, Hankow, Kuikiang, Chingkiang, Tientsin, Newchang, and Canton, which are not international, as is Shanghai, but directly controlled by British officials.

At Amoy the Consul in 1851 leased a piece of land

from the Chinese authorities, subsequently granting it for ninety-nine years to British subjects only. Our concession in that port is therefore leased from the Chinese under mutual agreement.

At Hankow, the scene of trouble in January last, and Kuikiang, adjacent to it, the concessions are held under leases dated March 21 and March 25, 1861, which stipulate for the payment of ground-rent to the Chinese Government, and contain a clause that as long as the ground-rent is paid the British Consul shall exercise sole control in allotting land, constructing roads, erecting buildings, and other matters.

The Newchang lease and that under which we hold Shameen—the British concession at Canton—provide for payment of an annual rent, and grant to the British "undisturbed possession so long as the rent hereby reserved shall be paid."

At Tientsin no formal lease was ever prepared, but here, too, ground-rent is paid annually, and the receipts of the Chinese authorities may be taken as consent to the terms under which we have held the concession for so many years.

It will therefore be seen that the British concessions were acquired under legal conditions.

In several cases the areas thus leased to or purchased by foreign Powers consisted of low-lying, swampy, and undeveloped land, which has since by initiative and enterprise developed into the present model towns. It required much time and patience; land had to be filled in, wharves to be built, and rivers dredged, before the areas were suitable for residence and trade. As time passed, modern methods of municipal administration and the security enjoyed by the population, Chinese and foreign, within the concession areas, induced numbers of Chinese banks, business firms, and others to purchase or rent property under foreign control. In each of the British concessions the Chinese population is much in excess of the white inhabitants. For example, at Shanghai the international settlement has a Chinese population of nearly one million. They appreciate that law and order, sanitation, and general living conditions are at a high level compared with a Chinese city, and the demand for houses created by the growing trade and increasing native population has resulted in a rise in property values within the concessions.

Shanghai, the most important international settlement in China, over which the first American Consul hoisted the United States flag in 1848, has an area of 5,590 acres, and the present value of land and property there exceeds £20,000,000. When it passed into international control it was a mud flat. To-day it is one of the great commercial cities of the world, possessing well-made streets, electric lighting, modern drainage, tramways, a Health Department, and an efficient police force. The outstanding loans and debentures of the Municipal Council, which is presided over by an American citizen, but on which British interests predominate, exceeded £6,000,000 at the end of 1924.

The foreign vested interests in this erstwhile mud flat developed by European enterprise now amount to £63,000,000, a sum in the main expended to foster British and foreign trade with Shanghai.

In Shanghai there are also forty-two native banks, owned, managed, and financed by Chinese, and dealing largely with foreigners. We also find 240;000 Chinese merchants within the boundaries of the international settlement, who are largely dependent upon foreign trade, and whose businesses have been built up under British or American auspices.

The story of the international settlement at Shanghai is typical of those elsewhere in China. The Anglo-French concession at Shameen, an island in the river off Canton, is a further example of development.

To satisfy the requirements of traders for accommodation in which they could conduct commerce apart from local conflicts, and to meet the objection that foreigners should not own property on Chinese soil, a mud bank in the stream was assigned to the traders. Canton remains to-day much as it was in 1843. It is a city of 2,000,000 inhabitants, shut in on three sides by a wall, and on the remaining one by the river. No city on earth has so large a population herded in so small a space. It is in striking contrast to Shameen, which has become a miniature modern town, with its hotel, palatial buildings, and warehouses, its fire brigade, waterworks, ice plant, and police force.

The standard of hygiene and comfort attained is the result of years of constructive energy, and we should only relinquish these concessions provided guarantees are given that the foreigner will be properly treated and afforded the usual trading facilities as in any civilised country.

The foreign concession has its value from the Chinese

standpoint, for when an official is deposed, or a military leader is defeated by another, he must perforce seek refuge in a quarter where there is a guarantee of safety. That assurance is found in the foreign concession, whither these anti-foreigners have no hesitation in turning a hurried step. At the moment the concession at Tientsin has three ex-presidents, and more than a dozen ex-war lords and other high officials, who have thus allowed the dictates of safety to overcome those of personal animus.

The British Government has already, in its Memorandum of December, 1926, agreed in principle to return of the concessions under joint control of China and the foreign inhabitants, when a stable government that can lay claim to real authority shall be established. Pending a responsible body with which to negotiate, our policy in the interim is clearly indicated in the declaration issued by the diplomatic body at Peking in February, 1927, regarding the position of the international settlement at Shanghai.

This declaration stated :

" In the light of military events which are at present taking place in the region of Shanghai, and which may at any moment have serious consequences for the safety of life and property of their respective nationals, as was apparent from the bombardment on the twenty-second of this month, the interested diplomatic representatives feel compelled to recall that the international settlement at Shanghai, like other concessions in China, was established in virtue of regular agreements with the Chinese Government, in order to make it possible for foreigners to reside there freely and carry on their trade.

" In the course of party strife of which the region has been the scene the authorities of the international settlement have scrupulously abstained from favouring any of the conflicting parties involved, and, in spite of the difficulties of the situation, they are maintaining in that respect the strict neutrality imposed upon them by the nature of the state of affairs thus established.

"The interested diplomatic representatives are thus warranted in expecting on the part of the Chinese authorities the observance of the same rule of conduct, and they look to the heads of armies involved to take all measures necessary to avoid incidents which would constrain foreign authorities themselves to take measures indispensable for insuring the safety of persons and property of their nationals."

Changes having been decided upon, and held in abeyance only because of the lack of responsible government authorised to speak for China as a whole, it is now only necessary to point out the dangers to be guarded against in altering a system which has in the past enriched alike Chinese and European.

We should also take into consideration the fact that opposition to the return of the concessions to Chinese control partly emanates from the Chinese population who live and flourish within their boundaries.

The latter have had the opportunity of comparing life in a purely native city with that in one governed by a foreign municipality. They realise that the besetting anxieties of existence for the ordinary Chinese trader— civil strife, erratic taxation, based on no plan and without regard to circumstances beyond the determination to raise money—are not found under foreign rule. Moreover, they are apprehensive that a change involving the placing of their interests into purely Chinese hands would stultify progress, and jeopardise the foreign trade on which their livelihood is mainly dependent.

That such fear is not illusory is shown by the fate of the ex-German and Russian concessions at Tientsin, restored to Chinese control after the Great War. On assuming control of these concessions, the Chinese Government announced its intention of forming them into model settlements ; they further promised that foreigners, who were the chief element in the population, should have a voice in municipal administration.

These promises have not been redeemed. The former German concession is administered by a subordinate police official, appointed by Peking, and attempts have been made to substitute leases of thirty years' duration for existing perpetual ones wherever a change in owner-ship of property has occurred. In both concessions not only has there been no foreign representation on the municipal council, but under orders from the governor of the province for the time being, a large portion of the taxes collected, which had hitherto been expended upon maintenance of roads and public improvements, has been confiscated for military uses. The late military commander of the district even increased the water rate and the charges for electricity to provide funds for his army. Conditions such as these, if extended to the other foreign concessions in China, would obviously have the most damaging effects on trade.

In view of the importance of Anglo-Chinese and Anglo-American relations in the future, I have dealt at length with the concessions as a vital organisation of the treaty ports through which there is a constant stream of commercial traffic.

The following figures demonstrate how considerable that trade is, and what its continuance and increase upon peaceful terms means to both China and Great Britain :

BRITISH GOODS EXPORTED TO CHINA AND HONG-KONG.

	1924 £	1925 £	1926 £
To China ...	20,346,613	14,633,399	16,426,858
To Hong Kong	8,554,434	5,109,808	3,181,586
	£28,901,047	£19,743,207	£19,608,444

1925 was conspicuous for the anti-British boycott, and a consequent fall of nearly one-third in the value of British goods imported, with a corresponding fall in Customs revenue derived from taxation of imports. Part of this depreciation, as regards goods entering China through the five ports of Shanghai, Tientsin, Hankow, Canton, and Dairen, was made up during 1926. On the other hand, the continued boycott of Hong Kong, ringed round by territory under the immediate sway of the Cantonese Government, is reflected in a still further depreciation in the value of goods imported into that colony for re-export inland.

This trade with China, and the large exports in tea, silks, furs, eggs, bristles, and other produce, were almost entirely carried in British ships, with a proportion of Chinese and Japanese vessels. The next in order of commercial importance is the United States, whose ships in 1925 carried four and a half per cent. of the total trade with China.

A study of the statistics of British trade with China reveals the significance of any appreciable decline.

The figures for 1926 are not yet available, but those for 1925 show that forty per cent. of the cotton goods sold in China were made in Lancashire. The following show Lancashire's exports of cotton goods and yarns to the world and China :

	World.	China.
1924	£199,162,166	£12,918,587
1925	£199,407,943	£7,661,596
1926	£154,343,161	£7,256,502

Moreover, sixty per cent. of all cotton goods landed at Shanghai during 1925 were of British manufacture.

To these figures is allied the fact that more than half of the 118 cotton mills, containing 21,000 looms, are equipped with machinery made in Lancashire. The close relation to China of one of our predominant British industries is therefore apparent.

Other figures for our export trade to China in 1925 include the following items :

Woollen tissues	£2,165,084
Worsted tissues	£626,500
Iron and steel	£1,586,425
Machinery	£1,190,399
Electrical goods	£353,751
Tobacco	£740,509

These are the main industries affected by the recent anti-British agitation in China, and the threat of future trade difficulties, whilst there are few industries of importance in the country that can afford to view with unconcern any rupture of our trade relations with China.

Were the Cantonese Government able to give effect

to its present aims, the conditions essential to the growth of our export trade with China would disappear, while present commerce would diminish considerably, apart from that of the United States, France, and Japan. The difference, however, between Great Britain and the other countries named is that, while trade with China is vital to our prosperity, to France and the United States it is still a "side line," and, although lucrative, is not essential to the industries catering for it.

United States trade with China began at Canton in 1784, but its growth has not kept pace with that of the American nation. The Great War diverted a considerable amount of Chinese trade to the United States, and assisted to overcome the handicap imposed by American neglect of trading opportunities with China in the past.

In 1896 the United States had 6·7 per cent. of the total foreign trade with China. By 1905 it had increased to 15 per cent., but in 1913, before the outbreak of war, the growing trade with Britain, Japan, and other foreign nations had reduced America's percentage to 7·6 of the total world exports and imports during that year.

Expressed in dollars the United States Chinese trade has expanded as follows :

			Imports	Exports
1913	...	...	41,387,000	31,956,000
1923	...	...	126,471,000	117,047,000
1926	...	...	149,962,775	103,400,354

The principal American imports from China are albumen, aniline dyes, cotton, vegetable oils, hides, and raw silk. Exports to China from the United States include iron and steel machinery, motors, railway material, chemicals, dyes, electrical machinery and materials, leather goods, paper products, mineral oils, and tobacco.

There is scope for considerable expansion of trade between the United States and China. The unpopularity of the Japanese in China, and the fact that in iron, steel, and chemical products Japan can hardly supply her own needs, will result in many articles formerly imported into China from Japan being replaced by Chinese-manufactured goods as soon as necessary factories are built. China will, therefore, need steel and iron products, electrical machinery and appliances, chemicals, and other articles, to modernise her industry in increasing quantity, the bulk of which must be supplied by the United States or Great Britain.

The industrial development of China depends in the first instance upon an increasing trade with those nations equipped to supply scientific aid and advice to meet her growing requirements ; there is a wide field open to their activities and China will need all their assistance from whatever aspect it is regarded.

Modern industrial development within the borders of China dates from about 1894, when the first Chinese cotton mills were erected at Shanghai and Wuchang. Prior to that year the only industries in the country, apart from agriculture, were the handicraft guilds, of which there are seventy-two in Canton alone. In some cases this handicraft work is in the hands of one family. Lacquer-work, for instance, is still carried on by a secret process known only to one particular household.

The most highly industrialised cities in China are Shanghai, Tientsin, and Canton, and the largest single industries are cotton mills, silk filatures, tanneries, match factories, rice and flour mills.

In Canton there are at present a cement works, the Electric Light Company's plant, ærated water factories, a flour mill, a tannery, about seventeen match factories, thirty rice mills, several dozen silk filatures, and some paper factories. With the exception of one ærated water factory, owned by a British firm, all these industries are dominated by Chinese capital.

The centre of the cotton industry is at Shanghai, although many mills owned by Japanese and Chinese have recently been erected at Tsingtao, Wuchang, and elsewhere. Only five mills, all situated at Shanghai, are British owned. Of the remainder, forty-five are Japanese, the balance being the property of, and operated by, Chinese employers.

Working conditions and wages in the British owned companies compare more than favourably with those under Japanese and Chinese control. The development of Chinese industry on modern lines, and the introduction of the factory system, coincided with the decline of the monarchy and of law and order generally. It is partly due to this that the state of industrial workers in China, when judged by British standards, needs drastic improvement. Feeble attempts have been made by short-lived Chinese Governments to regulate industry, but where reforming legislation has become law it has been more honoured in the breach than in the observance, and the absence of any system of factory inspection renders the regulation a dead letter. China is, in fact, a paradise for the employer, who can more or less fix the wage and work his employees for as many hours as the human body can endure toil, without interference from the State. The fact that to-day there are still only five British owned cotton mills in the whole of China, out of a total of 118, is clear evidence that British capitalists have not sought to take advantage of this state of affairs.

A beginning at factory legislation was made in 1923, when the Chinese Ministry of Agriculture and Commerce issued a Ministerial Order No. 223, which laid down, among other things, the following regulations :

" *Article* 3.—A factory owner shall be prohibited from employing boys under ten and girls under twelve years of age.
" *Article* 4.—Boys under seventeen and girls under eighteen shall be termed juvenile workers and employed only on light work.
" *Article* 6.—Excluding the time of rest, the working hours for juvenile workers shall not exceed eight hours a day, and for adult workers ten hours a day.
" *Article* 8.—Adult workers shall be given at least two days' rest per month, and juvenile workers three days' rest per month."

Other clauses of this order related to the settlement of wages in cash, the payment of overtime, and prohibition of work in unsanitary buildings. On the whole it was a modest instalment of social reform, designed to bring Chinese factory conditions into closer relation with

European standards. Unfortunately this order has not been enforced, and recent investigations and consular reports reveal industrial conditions in China to be amongst the worst in the world. It is probably only the low standard of living generally that enables Chinese employers to maintain working conditions which are a national blot, a state of affairs that would never be tolerated by any country with a Government able to enforce its decrees.

In one of the Canton match factories, for instance, a report prepared in 1924 shows that 200 workers were employed, mainly small children of both sexes and a number of women, with twenty to thirty men to do the heavy work. The output of this factory averages 18,000 packets per day. Only the men are regular employees and paid by the month, the remainder being paid daily by piecework. The children, whose task consists of stripping the match frames and packing the boxes, earn two coppers per tray of 120 boxes, and a fast worker can gain as much as 1s. 3d. per day. The report further states : " Women work faster, and can pack an average of thirty trays daily, but, owing to being frequently unable to work from illness, they are not so much to be depended on as child workers." The hours of work, it should be added, amount to twelve daily, seven days a week, holidays consisting only of the usual Chinese festival days.

The match factories are by no means exceptional. A recent report by an American secretary of the Chinese Y.M.C.A. narrates conditions in the silk filatures at Chefoo, where there are forty-two firms, employing from

20,000 to 30,000 men and boys, according to season. Each is paid by piecework and must handle 960 cocoons per day and produce eight skeins of silk, for which he receives forty Chinese coppers, or about 5½d. Food is provided in addition, but it is of poor quality, costing about 1½d. per day. The most rapid and skilled workers can finish their daily quota in ten or eleven hours ; others vary from twelve to fifteen hours. If a worker is unable to complete the allotted amount and obtain sufficient sleep within the twenty-four hours he is simply dismissed.

Investigations prove how essential it is for the introduction of factory legislation, but any move in that direction must be made with care and circumspection, for an attempt to change or modify working hours and conditions brings one into direct conflict with the heads of families who consider themselves entitled to control and exploit the members of those families by virtue of their mandate as rulers of the household.

The report goes on to say :

"The sanitary conditions in the silk factories are extremely bad. In order to protect the silk, the atmosphere must be kept warm and moist. Windows and doors are therefore continually closed, and the air is constantly loaded with odorous dust and germs. The workers almost universally wear no clothing above the waist. They can readily be recognised in any crowd by their sallow complexion. All workers must live in the factories. Those completing their work before night are free to go where they please, but they must return by dark. This means that only a few men get out of the factories except on special occasions. When they finish their work at night they pull out their roll of bedding and sleep on the floors, on stray boards laid across their benches, or on the ground in the courtyard. They rise at break of day, roll up their blankets and stack them in some corner until night. Thus they work, eat, and sleep in the same quarters.''

Factory conditions in Chefoo are, nevertheless, superior to those in many other Chinese cities, owing to the influence of Christian Chinese managers who endeavour to improve the state of affairs.

In the cinnabar mines of Honan, for example, entire villages—men, women, and children—are being slowly poisoned as a result of the conditions in which work is carried on. Yet no attempt is made, either by successive Governments or employers, to improve matters, and safeguard the workers from disease in a particularly hideous form.

A few years since the Rockefeller Institute carried out an investigation in Honan mines that are infested with hookworm, in one of which over eighty per cent. of those employed were suffering from the disease. Careful advice was given to the authorities by American experts, in order that the disease might be eradicated from the mines and countryside, but none of these recommendations was carried out, and to-day the same lamentable conditions prevail.

In all Chinese industries the employers exercise absolute control ; men are engaged and discharged at will. ''Workers' Councils '' and ''Shop Committees '' are unknown, and until the efforts recently made by Russian propagandists to initiate trade unions, there were no regular organisations of the workers in China. No provision is made for health, accident, or sickness insurance ; in fact, the lot of the worker in China is far worse than anything in the history of this country. It is an ironic comment upon the anti-foreign propaganda used to stir up those in Chinese-owned industries that the best working conditions are found within the foreign concessions.

The match and silk industries mentioned are not in any way exceptional in the hours worked, as the following figures for other industries show :

Hair-net factories (in which women are mostly employed), $8\frac{1}{2}$ hours a day ; straw braid, 10 to 12 hours a day ; peanut factories, 10 hours ; fish industry, 10 to 14 hours daily ; skilled artisans, 10 to 13 hours.

Turning to another province of China, we find that in Szechuan, with a population estimated at 60,000,000 to 70,000,000, none has ever heard of limitation of hours of labour, unemployment pay, factory regulations, or health services for employees. A feature of industrial life in this rich province has been the commandeering of labour by troops engaged in the civil wars. Consular reports show that even in the treaty port of Chungkiang gangs of men may be seen roped together with cords round their wrists, being carried off by soldiers to act as transport coolies, and no soldier in Szechuan ever carries his own baggage on the march. For this work the coolies receive no pay, but are presented with certificates giving them preferential treatment when the next commandeering takes place !

Compared with purely Chinese conditions, the workers

in Shanghai have little cause to quarrel with the foreign influence which governs the greater part of that city through the Municipal Council.

The labour movement in Shanghai, aiming at improved conditions, was initiated in 1916, and has progressed so rapidly within the past six years that there are now over eighty trade unions in the city, the chief of which are the seamen's and carpenter's.

These unions are largely subject to the influence of the Kuomintang party of Canton, and many are in receipt of funds derived from Russian sources. Despite frequent strikes, the majority of union leaders realise that but for the toleration shown by foreign employers their activities would have been suppressed and their organisations broken up.

In the record of Britain's trade relations with China it should be remembered that, while the industrial lock-out has been common in the country since the first Chinese owned factories were opened, trade unions and strikes are unknown in most parts of China, and have only become strong movements in cities where trade is mainly in foreign hands, which indicates that Western employers are more amenable to organisation for the protection of the worker than are the Chinese employers elsewhere.

Investigations with a view to reduction in the number of children employed in Shanghai cotton mills have already been made, and the following extracts from reports collected show the difficulty confronting those desirous of effecting improvement in that area :

The difficulties in the way of improvement clearly shown in these despatches, of which, perhaps, the greatest is that the Chinese worker is comparatively content with his lot, and as a rule considers himself fortunate if he has constant employment. Another is that the factories have developed along the lines of the old family industries, and as an instance of this may be cited the fact that the parents are unwilling to deprive themselves of the earnings of their children, and, having regard to the housing conditions prevailing in China, it is understandable that they like to be able to take their small children with them to the relative comfort of the mills. The fact that no arrangements are made to prevent accidents to these children from the machinery does not appear to the fatalistic Chinese temperament in the light of a serious defect, or as the neglect of an elementary principle of humanity on the part of their employers.

"Another difficulty is that the Chinese millowners will not make a move, and the foreign owners rather naturally decline to introduce revolutionary and probably unappreciated improvements, which would merely result in flooding the market with unemployed women and children, thus enabling their Chinese competitors to make radical cuts in pay, and so in the end render the lot of the workers considerably worse."

Despite these difficulties, the Commission on Child Labour appointed by the Shanghai Municipal Council has rendered good service to China by indicating in its report that the foreign authorities should at the earliest moment endeavour to give effect to the following recommendations :

1. Draft and enforce regulations prohibiting the employment in factories and industrial undertakings of

children under ten years of age, rising to twelve
years of age within four years from the date of the
regulations.

2. Prohibit the employment of children under fourteen
years of age for a longer period than twelve hours in
any period of twenty-four hours, such period of twelve
hours to include a compulsory rest of one hour.

3. Draft and enforce regulations under which every
child of under fourteen years of age should be given
twenty-four hours' continuous rest from work in at least
every fourteen days.

4. Prohibit the employment of children under fourteen
years of age in any dangerous place. It is also recom-
mended that the Council should provide an adequate
staff of trained men and women for carrying out the
duties of inspection under the regulations.

These are the reforms it was desired to introduce
when the anti-foreign propaganda made immediate
change in even the concession laws unwise. To
enforce this modest programme of reform within the
Shanghai international settlement alone would require
the approval of a majority of the consuls and ministers
of the treaty Powers, and of the ratepayers of the
settlement, most of whom are not of British birth. Even
with this majority assured, the new regulations would
only apply to a small part of the industries of Shanghai,
the greater portion of them being in purely Chinese
territory outside the settlement boundaries. Further, they
are owned by Chinese firms who show the strongest
disinclination to their factories being regulated by any
Government, Chinese or otherwise.

Speaking generally, the Chinese worker, with few

exceptions, labours both early and late, receiving in return a wage sufficient to keep body and soul together in a country where the general standard of living is the lowest in the world.

There are abuses of the gravest kind awaiting remedy in most of the industries, but in view of the superior conditions prevailing in the British owned factories it is difficult to see how a withdrawal of our traders would assist the Chinese working people, as some extremists declare.

The factory system has developed in China in times when there has been no sound Central Government able to enforce the necessary regulations, and employers are thus able to direct their factories without regard for the lives and well-being of their employees. Until a strong Government takes control and ensures enforcement of the present law, or until the labour unions in China are in a position to insist on sound conditions, the present state of affairs will continue.

An account of British and American relations with China would not be complete without reference to the Yangtse, the mighty river that cuts China in half and is open to steam navigation as far as Chungkiang, a British concession 1,427 miles from Shanghai. The Yangtse is the real heart of China, a barrier where the tide of internal rebellion has been so often rolled back. The Cantonese Government soon realised the importance of assuming control of this waterway, the campaign of 1926 culminating in the capture of Hankow, on the north bank, and removal of their capital and Government offices from Canton to that city.

Since 1883, when Mr. Archibald Little and Captain C. S. Plant made the first voyage from Shanghai to Chungkiang, the Yangtse has been the centre of an ever-growing trade between the two nations. Several of the British concessions are situated on the river, including Hankow, Kuikiang, Nanking, and Chinkiang. Together with Shanghai at its mouth, and trading posts at Ichang and other points in the interior, these ports have rivalled Canton as the centre of British interests in China.

The importance of our relations with whatever Government controls the Yangtse lies in the trade figures. These are not available in detail, but during 1925, 1,171 steamships entered the port of Chungkiang alone, with a total tonnage of 441,478.

In the farthest reaches of the river the number of steam vessels engaged in trade has increased from five in 1915 to sixty-two in 1926. Of these, nine were British owned, ten American, three Japanese, and the remainder Chinese.

The fact that British and other foreign ships have frequently been fired upon along the Yangtse since the beginning of the year is due to a certain resentment on the part of the river population to foreign shipping. Numbers of native boatmen formerly earned a meagre existence by towing native boats upstream. The advent of British and foreign steamers has eliminated much of this trade, and the livelihood gained from it by the Chinese rivermen.

While it is admitted that development of modern transport on the Yangtse is essential to increase of trade,

it certainly aroused local antagonism, and is regarded
as a violation of the river carriage monopoly held by
numerous families, in some cases for generations.

Owing to the hostilities of 1926, and present political
conditions in the rich province of Szechuan, both imports
and exports are now seriously curtailed. Since the
revenues derived from the Customs taxation depend
upon the resumption of trade it might have been expected that the Cantonese would endeavour to remove
the difficulties. The negotiation of the Hankow Agreement, however, and the handing over of the former
British concession there to the joint control of British
and Chinese ratepayers, has not improved matters.
Conditions on the Yangtse are now so precarious that
a complete withdrawal of all British subjects from the
Treaty ports on the river has taken place, with the
severance, at least until the present anti-foreign agitation has ceased, of all trading relations laboriously built
up by British, American, French, and other business
men in the region.

This means heavy loss to foreigners and Cantonese
alike, but at the present grave juncture in our relations
with China the choice lay between facing that loss or
supporting British traders with armed force, a step which
the Government, for practical reasons, deemed it undesirable to take, except at Shanghai, with its great
international interests.

If naval action to enforce our rights on the Yangtse
were decided upon it would be easier to bring pressure
upon the Cantonese forces than it was in January, for
the river rises rapidly in the spring, until a summer

8

level of 90 feet above the winter mark is reached. This enables cruisers to move up to Hankow, and river gun-boats to points beyond that are identified with British interests.

The question of what Britain stands to lose by severance or curtailment of the foreign relations is not fully answered by trade statistics. We must take into account the figures of British capital invested in China, and the progress of Chinese railways mainly under British direction and advice.

LOANS AND RAILWAYS

CHAPTER V

LOANS AND RAILWAYS

SINCE 1906 approximately £50,000,000 have been raised in London by Chinese Governments, of which £39,000,000 are still outstanding. Of this sum nearly one-half is guaranteed as to interest and repayment by the British supervision of the Maritime Customs revenue, which is security, or part security, for the following loans :

	Amount Outstanding on March 1, 1927.
	£
4 per cent. Gold Loan, 1895	3,719,101
5 per cent. Gold Loan, 1896	4,907,950
4½ per cent. Gold Loan, 1898	9,778,225
5 per cent. Reorganisation Loan, 1913 ...	24,224,600

The Boxer indemnity obligations are also secured on the Maritime Customs revenues, ranking immediately after the 4½ per cent. Gold Loan, bringing the total sum requisite to meet interest and sinking funds on these secured loans to over £7,000,000 per annum. After discharging this sum, the balance of revenues collected by the Imperial Maritime Customs is used by the Central Government to pay interest on internal loans and for other purposes.

The amount of China's unsecured foreign liabilities, other than British, in April, 1927, is :

				Chinese Dollars.
Japan ...	...	...	...	195,790,597·21
France ...	...	...	...	861,211·59
United States ...	...	...	29,218,145·49
Belgium	...	...	...	418,591·80
Austria	...	...	...	42,226,068·26
Denmark	...	...	...	293,077·22
Netherlands	...	...	...	1,078,379·43

(1 dollar approximately 3s.)

The total foreign indebtedness of China is approximately £150,000,000, of which about £39,000,000 are due to Great Britain. As regards British money, this was loaned on the understanding that capital and interest should be secured by revenues not subject to rival governors and military adventurers. Should British supervision be withdrawn, the only stable department of Chinese government that is efficiently administered will revert to a condition that has characterised Chinese finance in the past. The experience of the ex-German and Russian concessions at Tientsin, where money intended for local improvements has been appropriated for military purposes, would be the fate of the funds now available to meet the obligations arising from foreign debt.

In China taxes generally are farmed and local officials at liberty to exploit their district, and extract from the people as much as possible over and above the figure required to be paid into the central Treasury.

Until order is evolved out of chaos we are unable to gauge the extent of illegal exactions that have been going on since the rise of the Republic, but prior to 1911 the Imperial Government in Peking demanded £4,000,000 as the total annual contribution from the provinces. This did not represent the sum actually collected, which has been estimated by competent authorities at from £12,000,000 to £50,000,000. To this uncertainty in matters of taxation is partly due the small amount of trade in China, as distinct from dealings regulated through the foreign concessions that are not subject to intermittent and irregular collection.

The bulk of China's debt to Great Britain is secured by three national assets, the Imperial Maritime Customs, the Salt Administration, and the Railways, and any interference with those assets at once renders the safety of the loans illusory. The Gold Loans of 1896 and 1898 are secured, both as regards interest and principal, upon the revenues of the Maritime Customs, while the Re-organisation Loan of 1913, although in the first place a charge upon the Salt Administration, is also secured upon the Customs Revenues, subject to prior existing charges. The published figures show that for some years past the service of the Reorganisation Loan has been paid from this source.

In spite of statements that the receipts of the Imperial Maritime Customs are monopolised for payment of China's foreign debt, without any national benefit accruing, the latest figures show that of a net collection of approximately £12,000,000 per annum, only £7,000,000 are required for foreign debt service.

The Anglo-French Loan of 1908, to the extent of Kuping taels 2,350,000 per annum, and the Crisp Loan of 1912 are secured upon the Salt Gabelle, or taxation service, which was reorganised in 1913 under British auspices.

Shortly after the Republic became an established fact it was found necessary to negotiate these fresh loans, and as the revenue derived from the Maritime Customs was inadequate to meet the new charges involved, it was decided to exploit that obtainable from salt. Thus arose the Salt Gabelle, created by Sir Richard Dane, K.C.I.E., a monument to the constructive genius and ability of this official, who had already served with distinction in various excise and financial capacities in India.

As might be expected under such control, the revenue surpassed anticipations, furnishing to the Peking Government more than three times the sum required in liquidation of the loan charges. Recently this source of revenue has been seized, and the loans dependent upon it are consequently endangered.

In the next category are the Railway Loans negotiated in Great Britain, since China lacked not only railway experts, but also funds with which to construct the lines. They are secured by the receipts and assets of the railways concerned, but in the present state of China, with the majority closed to traffic for all except the unpaid transport of troops, and rolling stock falling into decay, the market value of the loans has depreciated.

These are the main outstanding debts between China and Great Britain, and they represent money invested in China, mostly by small investors, at interest varying from $4\frac{1}{2}$ per cent. to 6 per cent.—probably a lower figure than would have been charged elsewhere at the time the loans were negotiated.

As regards the state of various loans, the following are at present (April, 1927) in default :

Tientsin-Pukow Railway Five Per Cent. Loan of 1908. —*British Issue :* Interest in default from April 1, 1926. Only fifty per cent. of the principal due April 1, 1926, has so far been paid.

German Issue : Interest in default from October 1, 1924, and principal from April 1, 1925.

Tientsin-Pukow Railway Five Per Cent. Supplementary Loan of 1910.—*British Issue :* Interest and principal in default from November 1, 1925.

German Issue : Interest and principal in default from November 1, 1924.

Canton-Kowloon Railway Five Per Cent. Loan of 1907.—Interest and principal in default from December 1, 1925.

Hukuang Railways Five Per Cent. Gold Loan of 1911. —*British, French, and American Issues :* Interest and principal in default from June 15, 1926.

German Issue : Interest in default from December 15, 1925, and principal from June 15, 1925.

Honan Railway Five Per Cent. Gold Loan of 1905.— Interest and principal in default from July 1, 1926.

Lung-Tsing-u-Hai Railway Loan of 1913 (issued in Brussels).—Interest in default from January 1, 1926.

Chinese Government Eight Per Cent. Ten-Year Sterling Bonds of 1918 (known as Marconi Bonds).— Interest in default from August 28, 1921. Redemption was due to commence in August, 1924, but no repayments have yet been made.

Chinese Government Eight Per Cent. Sterling Treasury Notes of 1919 (known as Vickers Notes).— Interest in default from October 1, 1922. Redemption was due to commence in October, 1925, but no repayments have yet been made.

Railway mileage in China is approximately 7,000, compared with 36,849 miles in Great Britain and 265,000 miles in the United States. The principal railway systems are those linking Peking with Mukden, Hankow, and Suiyan, Tientsin-Pukow, Shanghai with Nanking, Hangchow, and Ningpo, Canton with Hankow and Kowloon, and the concessioned lines of the Chinese Eastern, the South Manchurian, and the Yunnan Railways.

Since the first railway at Woosung, built by foreign capital, was opened in 1876, twenty-five lines have been opened for passenger and goods traffic. A further twenty-nine have been planned in the south and interior, for which contracts were arranged, but the civil war has necessitated an indefinite postponement.

The outstanding obligations to foreign nations for completed railways built is £63,845,450. As already remarked, these loans are secured by the revenues of the railways concerned, and prior to the internecine warfare, the companies were not only able to meet the debt charges, but were in a position to allocate funds for expansion and replacement of rolling stock, while charging low traffic rates.

During the prolonged civil war railway revenues have largely disappeared owing to the compulsory transport of troops without payment, and the seizure of traffic receipts by military commanders. Rolling stock has been commandeered without compensation, and the lines used in accordance with the dictates of warring chieftains. It is estimated that upwards of £2,000,000, which rightly belonged to the holders of Chinese railway bonds, have been lost in this way.

A perusal of extracts from official reports will indicate how serious has been the interference with Chinese railway administration within the past year or two.

Canton-Kowloon Railway: "In July, 1925, in connection with the anti-British agitation, the British Engineer-in-Chief and staff were driven out of Canton to take refuge in Hong Kong, the line being left to run itself under inexperienced Chinese management. He returned in November, 1926, and, owing to the shipping strike, the line was able to make profits, and debts for salaries of staff and materials were wiped out or materially reduced. No trains were run to Kowloon, however, and after various delayed payments of interest on the loans due from the railway there was a complete default of interest payments at the end of 1925."

Shanghai-Nanking Railway: "In spite of interference by military operations during the first half of 1925, the total earnings on paper exceeded those of previous years, but a large proportion represents military traffic unpaid for, although the loan agreement stipulates for payment of military charges at half-rates in cash. The condition of the existing rolling stock on this railway is a pleasant contrast to that of other lines, and attempts to transfer it to other railways for military purposes have been frustrated."

Tientsin-Pukow Railway: "This line has suffered throughout 1925 from military depredations, and is now divided into two independent sections under separate military control. As a result the railway is deep in debt, and there has been a complete default in payments of interest charges on loans outstanding. The deterioration of equipment, especially locomotives, is very serious.''

Peking-Mukden Railway : '' While the earnings of this line were good during the earlier months of the year, civil war broke out again in the autumn, and it has since been a regular battleground. Damage done to the line in recent fighting was estimated at between £300,000 and £500,000. Numbers of locomotives were deserted by the staff and left to freeze.''

Nanchang-Kuikiang Railway : '' This line is now seriously in arrears with the payment of interest on its Japanese loans, which are said to amount to £2,000,000. The receipts in 1925 amounted to £150,000, or £20,000 less than the previous year, the decrease being due to civil war and bad trade.''

That these examples represent the existing state of Chinese railways is shown by a recent Government Report, prepared by Mr. A. H. George, Acting Commercial Secretary at Shanghai, in which occur the following comments on the present situation :

'' At the moment of writing most of the railways in China serve no other purpose than to provide transport for large numbers of troops uncontrolled by any central organisation. Ordinary commodities can only be transported at the price of exorbitant fees to military commanders for every car used, and even this source of revenue is drying up, as it becomes more and more impossible to obtain rolling stock for commercial purposes, and shippers are abandoning any hope of getting their goods carried by rail.

'' It is difficult to describe the state of deterioration into which the rolling stock of the great trunk railways

PEKING

The great Stone Dragon in front of the south entrance to the Forbidden City.

PEKING

The market at the Great Water Gate (Ch'ien Men).

have fallen, and it is little exaggeration to say that unless the present rate of disorganisation is rapidly arrested the equipment will disappear altogether, leaving only the tracks and road-beds.''

A Chinese expert has estimated the value of goods lost owing to the inability of the railways to transport them at £80,000,000, a figure considerably in excess of the actual cost of construction of all the railways in China.

Both the railway and telegraph systems of China were rendered possible by foreign loans, but there is ample scope for improvement. The poverty resulting from the prevalent civil strife prevents the carrying out of an extended programme of railway construction, and in any case it could not be undertaken without the further financial aid of London, New York, or Tokio. In view of the present anarchy and failure of existing lines to meet their obligations, it is unlikely that any foreign nation would grant a loan for railways exposed to the constant menace of confiscation and damage.

The bulk of material required for efficient maintenance must be purchased abroad, but in view of recent delays in payment for material already supplied the railway executives find it difficult to secure even tenders for further work. Indeed, some foreign firms now insist on payment before delivering machinery and material, whilst others charge enhanced prices to cover the greater risk involved from the various factions—those who regard the railways, legally the property of foreign shareholders, as their personal property, and both use the equipment and appropriate the funds without explanation or redress.

Even the pretence at maintaining a system of independent accounts, which had in the past provided a check on railway revenues, has now been abandoned. To-day those controlling the railways are subject to no such check, with the inevitable result that embezzlement and peculation are rife.

Since the beginning of the present century the railways of China have been nominally under the direct control of the Central Government at Peking. Actually, as I have shown, many of the lines have been seized by local military governors for personal use. Until a Government assumes office that is able to restore order out of chaos it is futile to expect foreign nations to sink more money in Chinese railways. The remedy, which must be forthcoming if existing lines are not to be brought to a standstill through lack of equipment, could be found in the Central Government taking over the loans and guaranteeing the interest by allocating part of the growing Customs receipts at the treaty ports, or by creation of a special fund controlled by financial advisers not identified with prevailing feuds in China.

A note may well be inserted here regarding the foreign Post Offices in China under the present system of extraterritoriality. These number :

Great Britain	...	...	12
France	...	...	13
Japan	...	...	124
United States	...	...	1 (in Shanghai)

They are located at centres of population and industry, but, except at Shanghai, are really unnecessary and could with advantage be abolished. The Chinese postal service is extremely efficient, is staffed to some extent by Europeans, and compares favourably with the foreign postal organisations, while the multiplicity of services is a grievance in the minds of many Chinese which should be removed as soon as possible.

THE NORTH AND SOUTH

CHAPTER VI

THE NORTH AND SOUTH

For the genesis of the present condition of China, with the seemingly endless swing of the pendulum between pretence at democracy and military dictatorship, with constant feuds between rival war lords and the almost inexplicable picture of pacifist China, whether North or South, democrat or dictator, relying solely on force to gain the ends in view, we must go back to the Chino-Japanese War of 1894.

This conflict, fought out in a Far East still remote in the popular imagination of the Europe of that day, and ending in the decisive defeat of China, marked the beginning of a real awakening of the Celestial Empire, which had slumbered for four thousand years.

The war itself was similar to many such conflicts recorded in Chinese history. The Empress-Dowager, at that time the real ruler of China, had spent most of the money raised to strengthen the defences of the country, and especially the Chinese navy, upon a new Summer Palace. At the beginning of 1894 China still believed it was possible to be both pacifist and peaceful, and two battleships, with some cruisers and torpedo-boats and destroyers, were considered to be all the force necessary to deal with any potential trouble by sea.

A Chinese empire adhering to this easy-going

doctrine fell a prey to well-equipped Japanese forces, and half the Chinese fleet was lost in the first battle of the Yalu. Next, Port Arthur surrendered, and the Chinese warships remaining afloat were destroyed at Weihaiwei.

I open the present chapter on the awakening of China at this point because, if the issue of the Chino-Japanese War was never in doubt, the results have been far more dramatic in their repercussions upon the history of the thirty years which have followed than was foreseen at the time.

What were these results? Pre-eminently, their defeat implanted for the first time in the minds of the Chinese autocracy a belief in force as the means of settling disputes, whether internal or with foreign nations. The war had shown the weakness of China, despite her huge population and ancient civilisation. It had also clearly revealed the strength of the European Powers— whose trade with China, notwithstanding drastic regulation, was growing—and of Japan, now becoming Western in outlook and fast developing her resources with European aid.

Another result of the war of 1894 was that Japan used her victory to establish her influence in Korea, and further demanded the cession of the Liaotung Peninsula, on which Port Arthur is situated.

The seizure of Korea, however, was sufficient to render more remote the chance of Russia realising her ambition for ice-free harbours in the Pacific. Thus did the Chino-Japanese War pave the way to the conflict between Russia and Japan.

A third result of this war, and one of especial interest at the present juncture in the story of China's awakening, was the fact that it marked the beginning of her foreign debt. To meet the indemnity demanded by Japan, China was forced to negotiate the first loan of £50,000,000 in Europe.

In three ways, therefore, it can be said that the war of 1894 signalled a new era in the history of China. Nor was the march of events opened up at that time long delayed. Three years later European intervention in the affairs of the ancient empire was emphasised by the leasing, under diplomatic pressure, of a number of ports by the Powers. Germany was in the van with her entry into Kiaochao in 1897. Britain went to Weihaiwei, and France to Kwang-chow-wan. Even Italy joined in the scramble for zones of influence, whilst Russia was already there.

Within the boundaries of China developments took the form so often found in the history of empires embarrassed by defeat. Demands for reforms, counter-moves by those in power against the reformers, a ding-dong fight favouring first one side and then the other, ending in a nation unprepared for democratic rule falling a prey to adventurous, and unscrupulous, leaders and political aspirants.

The first reforms demanded appear modest enough to the European reader, accustomed to the art of democratic government. Only two changes were urged on the weak Emperor Kwang Hsu by the Chinese reform party. These were (1) the reorganisation of the Government and (2) the founding of modern schools and colleges which would bring to China the educational facilities enjoyed in other lands, including Japan. But China was under the Manchu régime with centuries of despotic rule behind her, and cautious as this programme appeared, it was decided that if Kwang Hsu should initiate it, other and stronger hands must seize the reins of power and save China from the taint of "modernisation."

On September 22, 1898, the Empress-Dowager, thoroughly alarmed at the prospect, seized the Emperor and, under the pretext that he was ill, established a Regency.

Once securely in control, this determined woman, already sixty-five years of age, moved against the reformers, who, with good reason, promptly fled from Peking.

The departure of the Reform party, and the temporary eclipse of all they had accomplished with the halting aid of Kwang Hsu, did not lessen the counter-agitation against the whole idea of any change whatever. Indeed, it gathered impetus. Mohammedan troops from Kansu were brought east to garrison Peking, no liberal-minded advisers were tolerated, and these moves were followed by a decree from the Empress-Dowager announcing that the Emperor Kwang Hsu had abdicated and that, by request, she had consented to take over control of the country. The nomination of the infant son of Prince Tuan as the next Emperor completed, apparently, the ascendancy of the reactionaries.

As history has so often recorded, this policy of "sitting on the safety valve" brought in its train changes far more fundamental and vital than those against which the Empress-Dowager had, as she imagined, barred and bolted the door.

Three different forces were working, each in its own way, to put back the clock. There were the reformers of the Chinese Nationalist party, who included enlightened and capable men. There were the watchful eyes of the European Powers, who frowned on this attempt to stay the march of progress and sided with the reformers.

And lastly, as 1900 dawned, the first whispers came of another force called "Boxers," recruited from the adherents of gymnastic societies.

The Boxers were the force responsible for the unfolding of the next chapter in the slow stirring of Chinese nationality. They were antagonistic to both Europe and Japan and in opposition to an imperial family which was Manchurian rather than Chinese, the Manchus who were so far removed from the soul of the ancient civilisation of China that they regarded the Chinese as a conquered race.

The Boxer movement originated in Shantung, a province sacred as the birthplace of Confucius, a teacher whose precepts, as already remarked, have dominated a quarter of the human race for over two thousand years. Its adherents believed that Chinese reverses, the humiliations experienced at the hands of foreign Powers by a proud and ancient civilisation, had arisen from the presence of foreigners in their country. According to the Boxers, all China needed was to evict the Manchurian rulers in Peking, sweep out every foreigner, and found a new China free from the land-grabbers and

Western traders, with a real Chinese dynasty governing the people.

In pursuance of this programme they hastened to Peking, destroying railways and murdering 232 European and American missionaries and their children, whilst those of the Christian Chinese killed totalled several hundreds. Whatever savoured of progress and the foreigner was destroyed, while they marched as in ancient days to the tune of the drums of old China.

With wiser leadership the Boxers would have known that Nemesis must overtake them and their cause, for nothing made further foreign penetration into China more certain than the acts of murder and pillage against European subjects and missions.

The campaign of terrorism did not unseat the Empress-Dowager from the throne. But it brought the warships and forces of eight Great Powers into Chinese ports, and resulted in the guns of a foreign army being heard in Peking, whence the Empress-Dowager had fled in old clothes from the wrath of the avenging troops, taking with her the deposed Kwang Hsu lest any marauding reformer should replace him on the throne in her absence.

In that dark hour for her dynasty the cup of bitterness must have been full for even so strong a ruler as the Empress-Dowager. Hiding in Hsianfu, which had not sheltered the imperial throne for 1,300 years, she waited for the peace negotiations to reveal the fate of her personal power.

The final summing up, while imposing an indemnity and stringent guarantees against any renewed outbreaks aimed at the foreigner, went in her favour. Perhaps the European Powers remembered that three-quarters of China, including all the South, had remained outside the Boxer rising ; possibly they were pacified by the alacrity with which this woman meted out punishment to guilty governors and officials who had encouraged the outrages. But the indemnity, to be levied for thirty-nine years, was a blow almost beyond the financial capacity of the country, and promised further trouble for the ruling party.

The Empress-Dowager, for some time after the signing of peace, left the government to her officials, while she herself prepared to reverse her previous policy. She planned to institute a series of reforms designed with scant care and inquiry, but considered sufficiently attractive to secure for her the support of the powerful factions who disposed of much material for stirring up fresh agitation.

To me it has always seemed probable that from the suppression of the Boxer rising the Empress-Dowager realised for the first time her inability to stem the tide of progress which was carrying China along to new policies and new adventures. Sitting in the vastness of the Imperial Palace at Peking, she doubtless glimpsed the fact that not only was her power drawing to its appointed end, but that the dynasty to which she belonged—even the throne of the Son of Heaven—was destined soon to pass out of history.

Before the effects of these hurriedly conceived reforms could be ascertained, another blow was struck at China from beyond her borders. A band of Cossacks was attacked at Blagovestchenk, in Manchuria, and as a reprisal Russia sent a punitive expedition, which exceeded its authority and drove 2,000 inhabitants into the river, where they were drowned. This was followed by a Russian occupation of Manchuria.

The effects of such a move were far-reaching. Russia, who had seen her hopes of an ice-free port on the Pacific dwindling after the Chino-Japanese War of 1894, now believed her dreams to be nearing realisation. In addition, the seizure of Manchuria had increased her influence in the Far East, towards which the eyes of the Russian Czars had been turned for years, during which "Westernisation" had been deprecated in Russia just as it was still opposed by the reigning imperial family in China.

On the other hand, a Russia powerful in Eastern Asia was a standing threat to Japanese ambitions in Korea and elsewhere, and even to the safety of Japan itself. Diplomacy failed to adjust the conflicting interests thus arrayed against each other in the Pacific. Russia had reached Port Arthur, and the Japanese, fearful of her rising influence in the East, but confident in their own power, precipitated the Russo-Japanese War as the only settlement offering a promise of finality.

This campaign ranks as one of the most vital in the history of the twentieth century. For the first time an Eastern nation gained a decisive victory over a European Power on land and sea alike. All the endless trainloads of Russian peasants hurried along the Siberian railway to the slaughter around Port Arthur—the ice-free port gained after such efforts—did not prevent the Japanese from beating Russia to her knees. The Russian fleet, of indifferent constitution and morale, sailed round the world to meet the might of the new Japanese Navy in the China Seas, and was destroyed in the Straits of Tsushima.

In 1905 the Czar, alive to the murmur of the Russian people at these successive disasters, dramatically dropped the schemes for the supremacy of Russian influence in the Far East, and concluded peace on terms which, *inter alia,* included the evacuation of Manchuria and recognition of Japan's claims regarding Korea.

China took no active part in the war, although it was fought out on her territory. Her rulers, still scared by the aftermath of the Boxer rising, were forced to remain spectators in this crucial struggle between East and West, out of which came the slowly dawning consciousness of danger to China in a powerful "Westernised" Japan at her door.

The dramatic rise of Japan as a factor in the Far Eastern situation altered the whole outlook for China. The retreat of Russia from Port Arthur marked the limit of European influence in that country, just as the victory of Japan left her the strongest Power in the Pacific, and, from her land-hunger, the potential and formidable enemy of China.

This situation naturally reacted on the political situation within China. There was a renewed desire for reforms, drawn up on a more ambitious scale than that refused by the Empress-Dowager in 1898.

Dazed by the great changes in the distribution of power in the Far East, and anxious beyond all things

to keep China united, she bowed to the new agitation
and in 1906 issued a Reform Bill, which promised a
more or less democratic Constitution when the people
should be ready for it.

Indeed, she went further. More railways were
authorised, drastic changes were made in the system
of choosing officials by examination, which had existed
since 134 B.C., and a reform of the Chinese army, still
largely controlled by provincial governors, as in ancient
days, was instituted under the guidance of Yuan Shih
Kai, the Governor of Shantung, the province which had
seen the beginning of the Boxer trouble.

All China was in the melting-pot during those years
that followed the Russo-Japanese War. It seemed to
foreign observers that the Empress-Dowager was prepared to give way on most points, except the question
of the throne, to satisfy the reformers' demands.

Yet with this transition in progress they were not
satisfied. Intense distrust of the Manchus determined
them to sweep away the dynasty altogether and bring
into being a real democracy.

The reply of the Empress-Dowager to continued
agitation was to offer the reformers a national Parliament
in 1916. This move, tempting as it appeared at first
sight, was really an effort to postpone for another ten
years the evil day when the power would pass from the
throne. It was made in 1906, and those putting it
forward knew that much might happen before 1916
which would, were the reformers silenced, obviate the
trouble of honouring the promise when it fell due.

Had the Empress set about the task of modernising

THE NATIONAL UNIVERSITY, PEKING

the Manchu military organisation, called the Eight Banners, while there still remained time and opportunity, the plan to quieten the awakening masses by the offer of future democratic government might have saved the Manchu dynasty. But the Manchu military organisation in Peking continued to rely on bows and arrows, as they had done for centuries. The lessons of the war of 1894, and the more recent one between Japan and Russia, were lost upon the military advisers around the throne, with the result that, when 1916 dawned, not only had power passed into other hands, but the Son of Heaven, imperial ruler of China and occupant of the oldest throne on earth, had been swept away.

The Empress-Dowager died in 1908 at the age of seventy-five, her death taking place somewhat dramatically, for a few hours before the end the deposed Emperor, Kwang Hsu, expired in circumstances that were never, I believe, fully explained.

The Empress on her deathbed had decreed that the throne should pass to Kwang Hsu's nephew, Hsuan Tung, then a child of three, and that a Council of Regency be set up to govern in the spirit of the reforms she had planned until he became of age.

There now followed a scramble for power between the reformers and reactionaries, who, it was thought, wished to preserve the monarchy at all costs. The most influential of these in the Council of Regency was Yuan Shih Kai, the Governor of Shantung, who had been planning to reorganise the army.

The Imperial Senate, the first step towards democratic government promised by the late Empress-Dowager, met in 1910, and showed itself strongly in favour of the reformers and their plans for quickening the march of progress.

Yuan Shih Kai, as their leader, was rapidly gaining power, and on the ground that he had been concerned in the death of the Emperor Kwang Hsu, was forced to leave Peking. He retired to Shantung, and there awaited the opportunity for which he had been actively working.

In May, 1911, a Council of Ministers chosen from the Senate took over the reins from the Grand Council, which had hitherto conducted the administration of the country and contained men of experience and judgment. This change threw the country into further disorder, but it enabled the reactionaries, who dominated the infant Emperor, to assume a decisive attitude in the conduct of affairs.

More changes followed, but now aiming at strengthening the power of the throne. It was decreed that railways built in China would come under control of the Council of Ministers, and that new lines were to be constructed by that body.

The import of this move was obvious to all who knew China. In that country the railways were considered of primary importance for the rapid movement of troops to any part of the empire, and only incidentally as a means of transport for civilians and merchandise. By securing direct control over the railways the Central Government were in a position to rush an army to any part of the country that threatened revolution.

The real significance of this development was not lost on the growing numbers of educated Chinese and students who aimed at really democratic government. It meant the strengthening of Peking and the "old party," and discounted from its inception the importance of the opening of China's first Parliament, already fixed for 1913.

Whether the Chinese were really a democratic people, as the reformers believed, and whether the change over in a few years from absolute monarchy to Parliamentary government was in the interests of the country, or even a wise step, are questions to which only carefully qualified answers can be given at the present time.

It is true that, socially and industrially, the Chinese have for centuries been a democratic people. In China nothing ever prevented a boy of natural talent and industry rising from the lowest occupation to the highest office in the land.

But it will be seen, as we trace the course of events during the past fifteen years, that something more than the absence of any rigid caste system is necessary if a vast country, embracing millions of many creeds and in varying stages of development, is to make a success of democratic government. Self-discipline, a sense of civic duty, breadth of view, a well-informed public, stability of character—all these things depend upon the slow march of years. They cannot be imported overnight. In China, then on the verge of the great experiment, the growing-pains were destined to be severe.

Faced with a reactionary group around the throne bent on strengthening their military resources in order to dominate the promised Parliament before it had met, the dissatisfaction rapidly spread. The Russo-Japanese

War had revealed to the Chinese mind, and particularly its students, how a well-armed and determined force can defeat one that has no definite plan of campaign. The reformers decided that the time had come to expel the Manchus, to clear away the cliques around the throne who side-tracked every effort towards democracy, and, by proclaiming a republic, give self-government to China. With that decision there followed the revolt of 1911.

It began in Szechuan, the first explosion being due to popular opposition there at the passing of the railway to connect it with the Yangtse into the control of the Peking Government.

The rebels scored a series of rapid successes, including the capture of the important cities of Wuchang, Hankow, and Hanyani. The Council of Regency in Peking, caught without any plan, sent for Yuan Shih Kai and appointed him High Commissioner of the naval and military forces.

Yuan Shih Kai was able to stem the further advance of the armed reformers, but, the terms of settlement being left to him by a Regent who wanted peace at almost any price, he disclosed his real sympathies by allowing the apparently beaten rebels to practically dictate terms.

A fresh demand for a democratic constitution now came from three of the imperial Generals in the field, this timely request enabling Yuan Shih Kai to form a Cabinet in place of the deposed Council of Ministers.

The revolutionary forces continued to augment after the actual fighting had ended. The blunt demand made to Yuan Shih Kai by his own supporters for a republic was in the main approved by the provinces, who now gave their adherence to the movement.

Before the fate of the throne had been decided, events took a dramatic turn with the appearance at Canton of Sun Yat Sen, who had been in Europe when the revolution broke out. His advent was followed by a declaration setting up an independent Republican Government for Southern China, with its capital at Nanking and himself as first President.

This announcement was published to the world on January 1, 1912, and it found Yuan Shih Kai unprepared to meet the new challenge. The Treasury at Peking was empty, there were murmurs among some of the Northern troops which suggested that his popularity was waning, and famine in Central China.

For these reasons Yuan Shih Kai wisely decided against fresh hostilities to crush this new and spectacular defiance of the Manchu dynasty, which he still—nominally, at any rate—supported. Probably he knew that China's days as an empire were already numbered. From the moment when Sun Yat Sen's declaration divided China into two camps he turned his attention to clearing away the imperial tie, and thus opening the road to a reunion of Canton (South) and Peking (North) under a republic.

The final attempt to check the course of events was made by the widow of the Emperor Kwang Hsu, who visited Yuan Shih Kai, bearing in her hand the patent of nobility of a marquess, and, with the exception of the ducal title borne by descendants of Confucius, the highest honour in the gift of the Chinese Emperors. She offered it to the dictator if he would save the imperial throne. The offer was declined. It was proffered a second time, and again refused. There was to be no reprieve for the dynasty, which had outlived its welcome.

The end of the Chinese monarchy came on February 3, 1912, when the Manchu dynasty, which had withstood all attempts of foreign enemies to dislodge them, abdicated after signing a secret edict giving full power to Yuan Shih Kai.

The final phrases of the edict of abdication were :

"We hereby proclaim to the Imperial Kinsmen and the Manchus, Mongols, Mohammedans, and Tibetans that they should endeavour in the future to fuse and remove all racial differences and prejudices and maintain law and order with united efforts. It is our sincere hope that peace will once more be seen in the country and the people enjoy happiness under a republican government."

With those words the Son of Heaven, who had "reigned over all beneath the sun," and whose forbears had occupied the imperial throne of China since 2752 B.C., handed over the government of China to the rising tide of democracy.

During forty centuries numerous dynasties had occupied the throne of China. The Manchus, the last of these, had ruled from A.D. 1644 until 1912. Effete and corrupt for years, and aliens in the eyes of China, their passing was no loss to the country. For generations they had stifled instead of fostered the national aspirations of the Chinese people, for whom they had scant sympathy. From first to last they regarded their subjects as a conquered race—a fatal mistake when dealing with a proud people.

The immediate effect of the overthrow of the monarchy was what Yuan Shih Kai had hoped. Sun Yat Sen, the self-styled "President" of Southern China, resigned two months later in order to assist him in the unification of North and South.

The new President of China needed assistance, for, with the coming of power, his troubles had multiplied in that mysterious way known so well to all those generals and governors who have sought to rule in China. A proposal for removal of the capital to the South was settled by its remaining in Peking, and a mutiny among the Government troops was suppressed.

More difficult to adjust was the problem of finance. The Treasury was empty. Money was urgently needed to pay the troops and officials, and the only way to secure it, and quickly, was to borrow from abroad. The new powers in China were, however, opposed to foreign loans, since they implied foreign supervision and a tangible hold upon the security.

Yuan Shih Kai was forced to bow to the logic of events; the foreign loans were obtained, enabling the Republican Government to function while a National Advisory Council was formed of five representatives from each province, and five from the dependencies of Tibet, Mongolia, and Kokonor.

This Council survived for only one year, and in 1913 the first National House of Parliament met for the purpose of confirming Yuan Shih Kai as President.

China's first attempt at Parliamentary government,

promised years before by the Empress-Dowager, began in unhappy circumstances, for a few hours before the first meeting the leader of the Kuomingtang, or extreme Republican party at Canton, was assassinated when about to take the train for Peking.

The public excitement and tension arising out of this event had not died away before further trouble arose between North and South, due to a growing belief among the extremists in Parliament that Yuan Shih Kai was bent on becoming a military dictator now that he controlled Peking, and with it the money derived from taxation.

The second revolt of 1913 was suppressed, and, as President, Yuan Shih Kai proceeded to take even wider powers into his hands. Among the measures initiated to knit China closer to the Central Government was the appointment of military governors to each province over the civil authority. This development, following the revolt of 1913, is of more than passing interest for those who would understand the China of to-day, for up to that time she had been a nation in which the military were held in contempt. Soldiers were grouped with servants in the eyes of society. By this decree the civilian governors, hitherto holding supreme power, stepped down for the first time in history, and soldiers were appointed above them.

The first National Parliament of China, never more than a phantom legislature, was dissolved the following year, when an Advisory Board was set up in its stead, most of its members being chosen from Yuan Shih Kai's supporters. At the same time the provincial councils were abolished, and still greater powers were taken by the man who was now the virtual Dictator of China.

A remarkable feature of the new authority assumed by the Central Government was the "Constitutional Compact," by which the President remained in office for ten years, at the end of that term his successor to be chosen from three persons nominated by the retiring President. It is doubtful if such an arrangement would have been accepted by any party, however reactionary, in any other country in the world. It was obvious from the day when the "Compact" was announced that the only effect of this decree would be to stereotype for a generation the type of mind which would reign at the Presidency. Yuan Shih Kai could be relied upon, when his term ended, to either seek re-election or put before the Advisory Board three names of men, each of whom would continue the policy laid down by his predecessor. Yet such was the popularity of the President at that time, and the intellect of his opponents, that the "Compact" was accepted by those who claimed to speak for the Chinese people.

Thus matters stood on the outbreak of the Great War, a conflict that had barely started when China became the scene of one of the most sensational diplomatic moves of our generation. This was the Japanese bid for domination in China and the Far East by the presentation to the Peking Government of an ultimatum in the form of the famous Twenty-One Demands.

The moment for the launching of this bombshell was well chosen. The Allied Powers, who, with the United States, had always resisted any spread of Japanese influence in China, were engaged in a life and death struggle with Germany and Austria, which left them little time for other matters. Japan, early in the war, had, with the help of British troops, driven the Germans from their treaty port of Kiaochao, and, after the departure of the former, remained in sole occupation of that port.

When, in January, 1915, this document was suddenly presented at Peking, it was clear Japan intended to forestall any possible partition of China among whichever set of European Powers might prove victorious in the war.

Fearful of the continued presence of Japanese troops at Kiaochao, China informed Japan that permission to use the province of Shantung, in which Kiaochao was situated, for military operations would be withdrawn, since with the departure of the Germans the necessity for any warlike movements had disappeared.

Japan replied to this claim to quit Chinese soil by regarding the demand as an indirect slight, and forthwith presented her Twenty-One Demands, divided into five groups. This document, given acceptance in its original form, would have allowed Japan virtual control over the Chinese Empire. It was handed to Yuan Shih Kai with the utmost secrecy on the night of January 18, 1915.

It aimed at the elimination of European and American influence ; no document in history was ever so drastic or struck more directly at a national sovereignty.

An ominous sign, to those acquainted with the methods of Oriental diplomacy, was the fact that the paper on which the demands were set out had for its water-marks warships and machine-guns—a significant fact in a world where hints or suggestions are more usual than direct diplomatic statements.

Had China accepted the Japanese demands she would henceforth have had no hope of developing her own political life under either monarch, dictator, or parliament. They meant that at every turn her external affairs, and even her domestic life, were to be controlled by the Japanese. Certain of the clauses laid it down that Japan should henceforth build Chinese rail-ways, Japanese subjects should have the right to own land in Mongolia, and to work mines in Manchuria and Mongolia. The Japanese were to be consulted in matters regarding financial affairs and in the adjustment of ques-tions relating to police or military in those areas. It was further stipulated that the lease by which the Japanese owned Port Arthur should be renewed, and China was not to cede any land or port on her coastline to another foreign Power.

More fatal to Chinese national aspirations than even these provisions, however, was the list of demands set out in the notorious Group 5 of the document.

These were never put into operation, but they are sufficiently important, in any study of the Chinese question, to set out in full.

Group 5 contained seven articles as follows :

Article 1.—The Chinese Central Government shall employ influential Japanese advisers in political, financial, and military affairs.

Article 2.—Japanese hospitals, churches, and schools

in the interior of China shall be granted the right of owning land.

Article 3.—Inasmuch as the Japanese and Chinese Governments have had many cases of dispute between Japanese and Chinese police to settle, cases which cause no small misunderstanding, it is for this reason necessary that the police departments of important places (in China) shall be jointly administered by Japanese and Chinese, or that the police departments of these places shall employ numerous Japanese, so that they may at the same time help to plan for the improvement of the Chinese Police Service.

Article 4.—China shall purchase from Japan a fixed amount of munitions of war (say fifty per cent. or more) of what is needed by the Chinese Government, or that there shall be established in China a Chino-Japanese jointly worked arsenal. Japanese technical experts to be employed and Japanese material to be purchased.

Article 5.—China agrees to grant to Japan the right to construct a railway connecting Wuchang with Kui-kiang and Nanchang, another line between Nanchang and Hanchow, and another between Nanchang and Chaochou.

Article 6.—If China needs foreign capital to work mines, build railways, and construct harbour works (including dockyards) in the province of Fukien, Japan shall be first consulted.

Article 7.—China agrees that Japanese subjects shall have the right of missionary propaganda in China.

Despite the preoccupations of the war, when the terms of this ultimatum leaked out it caused an immediate and grave reaction of world opinion against the Japanese Government. Japan, realising that even a European war might not prevent the intervention of other Powers, and especially the United States, which was then neutral, promptly denied that the original demands had been as sweeping as suggested, and gave to the world a revised version, in which the objectionable articles had been deleted. Later they admitted that those in Group 5 had figured in the original document, but declared they were only intended as suggestions.

The demands, much modified, were pressed upon Yuan Shih Kai and his Advisory Council, and accepted on May 11, 1915. By this success Japan gained concessions from a phantom and unrepresentative Government, but it is important to remember, in view of what has followed, that at no time were the Chinese people consulted in the matter. Had any form of plebiscite been possible, it is certain that the demands would have been rejected by the nation.

Events were not long delayed after this diplomatic affront to China. Yuan Shih Kai had now become a convert to the system of monarchy which he had overthrown a few years before, and propaganda was begun emphasising the fact that China under an emperor had won prosperity until the decay of the alien dynasty had set in a generation or two before. "Elect a strong man for your emperor," whispered Yuan Shih Kai's emissaries, "and China will once more be strong and powerful and able to overthrow all her enemies."

At the appropriate moment Yuan Shih Kai called upon the provinces to vote on the question of whether or not he should abolish the Republic and be installed as the first of a new line of emperors. Bribes, judiciously distributed in the right quarters, resulted in heavy voting for the crowning of the erstwhile "President," and the coronation was fixed for February, 1916.

In laying his plans Yuan Shih Kai had apparently forgotten one thing. He had overlooked the possibility of intervention by the Japanese. Perhaps he felt this was a risk with which he could deal, and that Japan's threats would never be followed by action so soon after her rebuff over the recent Twenty-One Demands.

Actually it was an insurrection fomented by Japanese propaganda against him that brought about the collapse of his schemes. The rising began in Yunnan and spread rapidly. After some fighting, he yielded to the threat, and, abandoning the plans for his coronation, announced the formation of a Cabinet to maintain the Republic. By this time, however, there were powerful parties in the land which had lost faith in his passion for democracy. These groups declined his offer, and in the South a number of provinces declared their complete independence of the Central Government, forming a Southern Republican Confederation at Canton, the scene of Sun Yat Sen's former attempt to organise the South as a separate unit.

Before Yuan Shih Kai could move against this new menace to his personal power he died—on June 16, 1916—and thus passed the first President of the Chinese Republic, and the Governor whom, distrusted first by the Emperor and later by the people, nevertheless managed to maintain his personal ascendancy to the last.

Yuan Shih Kai found no easy task during his years of office in Peking, and the measure of his success may be judged by the fact that China was afflicted with no fewer than five Presidents in the eight years following his death.

With Yuan's demise power passed to Vice-President Li, his right-hand man, the newcomer being immediately faced with civil war between the Canton Nationalists, as the Southern Confederacy now styled itself, and the Peking Government. This renewed internal chaos gave further opportunity to a European Power to strengthen her hold on the Far East at the expense of a distracted China. France, who desired to extend the treaty territory at Tientsin, seized Lao Shih Kai. This action may, or may not, have had some connection with the fact that the Chinese openly favoured the German traders.

A new figure now makes his appearance on the Chinese stage. This is Tuan Chi Jui, a man of influence with the military governors, who opposed President Li for control of the Peking Government, and demanded that China should declare war on Germany.

To settle the deadlock between these rivals, a third leader, Chang Tsun, a thorough-going reactionary, was called in at Peking as mediator. He promptly dismissed what was left of the Cabinet, and paved the way for a triumph of the military party over the constitutional advisers of President Li.

This passing of power into the hands of the military was followed by yet another revolt in the South, always the most democratic centre of the country, but it did not prevent Chang Tsun from carrying out his real purpose—achieving a *coup d'état* and placing the deposed Emperor, still a young man, once more upon the Dragon Throne.

This mock restoration was carried out by a force of some four thousand badly equipped troops, who entered the palace at daybreak and seated the boy Emperor upon the throne. There followed one day's fighting, and with the setting sun the farce was over and the Emperor had disappeared again into the retirement from which the scheming Chang Tsun had dragged him.

Tuan Chi Jui now united the Northern Generals and re-established the Republic. A new Parliament was elected in August, 1918, while the members of the dissolved legislature met in Canton as a rival body, with Sun Yat Sen as their leader. The new President now tried, with more patience than success, to bring about a union between North and South. Negotiations resulted in an armistice, and a conference was held at Shanghai, but no agreement was reached.

Thus China slowly relapsed into the long drawn out battle between North and South which has been the dominating factor in that country for the past eight years.

The continuation of the senseless civil strife caused power to pass completely into the hands of the military, once and for so long subordinate to the civil governors. Opium was exploited to play a part in raising revenue for military adventures. A revolution broke out in Tibet, and plague in Manchuria.

At this moment in her history, when world opinion and the Chinese people realised that democratic government had created more abuses than it had cured, China—or that part controlled by Peking—sent delegates to the

MARSHALS CHANG-TSO-LIN AND WU PEI-FU

Peace Conference at Versailles. For the first time in history the representatives from the most ancient empire sat side by side with those of the Great Powers of both Old World and New. China expected much at Versailles. Had she possessed internal peace and a strong Central Government, she might have secured a new prestige and dignity—have definitely taken her place in the comity of nations, as Japan had done a generation before.

Unfortunately for China, and, I think, for the world, she was disappointed. The German lease of Kiaochao, on the return of which China had counted, was transferred to Japan. Her representatives had to return from the Peace Conference to report that even the one piece of "unredeemed China" at the gift of the Conference had been handed to a foreign Power.

The effect of this failure on the political situation was quickly revealed. Anti-Japanese riots broke out on a large scale. Tuan, sensing the hostility against him, formed the Anfu party to consolidate his hold on Peking, the possession of which city still meant control of most of the revenues. Chihli and Fengtien revolted against him, and Wu Pei Fu, their leader, defeated the Anfu forces, a victory which was followed by the rise to power of Chang Tso Lin, who obtained control of the Central Government in Peking in 1919.

The rise of Chang Tso Lin brings Chinese history to a new phase. The never-ending battle between North and South was now in full swing, and China was destined to pass through many weary years of civil war before any government arose strong enough to force its writ upon all parts of the country.

During this period of chaos into which the nation was entering two outstanding figures appear—Chang Tso Lin in the North and Sun Yat Sen in the South.

Sun Yat Sen, a professional revolutionist and a remarkable figure in modern Chinese history, was first driven out of Canton by the Kwang-Si faction, and then, in 1921, elected President of the Chinese Republic by the Southerners, although his authority never extended beyond the South.

Chang Tso Lin remained firmly in the saddle until 1922, when he quarrelled with Wu Pei Fu, a rival Northern leader, and a new civil war broke out, in which Chang was beaten.

Shortly after this defeat of the Northern dictator, Sun Yat Sen was once more overthrown in the South.

The national break-up had reached its final phase; the old unity had gone, and the fire of a new and robust nationalism destined to replace it was smouldering unseen in the pulsing heart of China. But the new forces were already there, and after 1922 the struggle between North and South took a new and definite form, focusing world-wide attention on the problems involved.

THE PRESENT CRISIS

CHAPTER VII

THE PRESENT CRISIS

THE story of China from 1922 to the present day is a pitiful narrative of a great civilisation, more ancient than that of Greece or Rome, as old as the civilisation of Lower Egypt, crumbling into final ruin. A record of civil war without end, of slow disintegration, which by the inexorable working of events has made once-proud imperial China the cockpit of conflicting forces, from which the European Powers, earnestly as they desired peace after their own wounds in the Great War, could not hold aloof. Had they done so, free play would have been allowed for the looting of their property by mobs, and their people, engaged in missionary and hospital work, or peaceful trade, first embarrassed, then openly insulted, and finally attacked, would inevitably be forced to leave behind their worldly goods and quit. This quite apart from the worldwide economic and political consequences involved.

Up to 1925 there was hope that either North or South, Peking or Canton, would prove sufficiently strong to re-unite divided China, and give it stable government. In the north, Chang Tso Lin, the Manchurian war lord, had at his back the legions of Manchuria, descendants of the warriors who had conquered China six centuries before, and founded the Manchu dynasty. Chang Tso

Lin was reputed to be a capable soldier and a "strong man" of the type that had often saved China from disruption in the past. Moreover, the Chinese masses had been accustomed by centuries of despotic, almost patriarchal, authority to look to one man for guidance and government.

So, no doubt, reckoned Chang Tso Lin when, securely in possession of Peking, he heard that the Kuomintang party, formed by Sun Yat Sen into a Southern Republic in Canton, intended to dispute his authority and engage him in civil war.

Events might have gone in his favour had not the Cantonese Republican Government taken a step without parallel in the history of the Chinese Empire. This was the despatch of a "mission" to Moscow, and the formation of a close alliance between the Southern Government and the Russian Soviet—the first occasion on which any Chinese party, rebel or otherwise, had concluded an alliance outside the borders of China.

The appearance of Bolshevik emissaries in Canton, bent not only upon imposing a Republican Government impregnated with their own opinions, but also upon destroying the powers and privileges possessed by the "capitalist" nations of Europe in China, strengthened the Southern Government. It gave them advisers of every kind. Russian officers undertook the training of their armies, Russian artillery, machine-guns, ammunition, rifles, were poured into China to strengthen the Soviet allies. With this material assistance came Red propagandists, who infected both Canton Government and people with the virus of Bolshevism. They preached the doctrine that the foreigner had for centuries battened on the poverty of the Chinese masses, a doctrine which will be exposed for the falsehood it is in my next chapter.

Strikes followed, a boycott was proclaimed that held up the entire trade of Hong Kong for months, "incidents" occurred in which foreigners were fired at and British ships captured, for all the world as if China was at war with the British Empire. Emboldened by early successes, and perhaps by the studied moderation of the British Government, anxious to meet the demands of the Nationalists as fairly as possible, the Canton Reds drew up a list of "demands," including return of all concessions leased to foreign Powers by previous Chinese Governments, and the withdrawal of all foreign officials, police, and others upon whom rested the task of maintaining law and order therein.

These demands, enforced only by words at first, but later, at Hankow and elsewhere, by violence, led inevitably to reluctant action by the European Powers, and to the despatch of British warships and a defence force of several thousand men to defend Shanghai and other threatened points. The United States, Japan, Spain, France, Italy, and Portugal were forced to take similar measures for safeguarding the lives of their subjects in the treaty ports. Thus the Southern Government at Canton was, at the beginning of 1927, brought to a point at which it must either ignore the counsel of its Russian advisers, or face the prospect of imposing its many demands by force upon Europe, in addition to completing the still unfinished task of conquering

Northern China and driving. Chang Tso Lin from Peking.

Much that is interesting had happened, however, before the intervention of Bolshevik Russia in the cause of the Cantonese Government paved the way to combined European action.

From 1922, where the account in the previous chapter ended, to 1924 the story of China is a record of continued intrigue and plot, of the rise and fall of first one party and then another. North and South seemed destined to pursue different roads, and both sides in the civil strife were in no mood for compromise.

Tuan Pao Chi, whose Presidency of China ended in July, 1924, settled the agitation against the Roman Catholics, and matters outstanding since the Great War with Germany. During his term of office another important step, alike for China and the whole world, was taken by the return of Russia to a voice in Far Eastern affairs, following the completion of an agreement signed by Wellington Koo on behalf of the Peking Government, and Karakhan for the Russian Soviet. For the first time since her defeat in the war with Japan, the voice of Russia, and of a Russia more bent upon fomenting trouble than any Czar of the past, was now to be heard in the councils of those in whose hands lay the destinies of China.

Wellington Koo became acting Premier for a few weeks, and then, in his turn, disappeared to make way for Dr. Yen.

Dr. Yen always gave me the impression of being a leader possessing far more character, in the Western sense, than those who have since followed him. That opinion was shared by the officials of other foreign Governments who had dealings with him.

Dr. Yen distrusted political cliques, and disliked government by plotting, such as had been the rule in Peking, particularly since the fall of the Manchu dynasty. His procedure more closely resembled British methods in Egypt. He chose his advisers on their merits, and announced that the vital task awaiting his Government was to improve Chinese relations with foreign Powers and strengthen her finances.

To those lacking an intimate acquaintance with China it will appear strange that with open rebellion over Southern China, and an unrecognised Government at Canton, Dr. Yen did not proceed to end the civil war in victory for the Northern forces at all costs. He acted wisely, however, in first undertaking the improvement of foreign relations and central finances.

So vast is China in area, so numerous in population, and so lacking in means of communication, that often in her history one or more provinces have been in open rebellion, often for years, without it having any appreciable effect either on the power, wealth, or prestige of the reigning emperor. As long as the national revenues were paid to the Central Government at Peking, the fact that several southern provinces refused to co-operate in the government made very little difference.

On the other hand, upon cordial relations with foreign Powers depended those very revenues which provided the war chest in Peking, and financial stability was an essential preliminary to win over the South and unify the country.

Further, Dr. Yen recognised that in his country support inclines naturally to the winning side. A wealthy and settled Government in Peking, with its army paid promptly, and on terms of friendship with foreign traders, would have a comparatively easy task in subduing the South, more particularly when the latter realised the new and unaccustomed state of affairs in the North, in striking contrast to their own Government, which was, until the arrival of funds from Moscow, on the verge of bankruptcy.

That plan might have succeeded, in spite of Russian gold, but for a new move by Chang Tso Lin, who in 1924 suddenly announced the formation of a separate Government of his own creation at Mukden, the capital of Manchuria. The immediate result of this fresh split was the diversion of part of the revenue due to the Central Government from Manchuria to Chang, who also declined to allow the agreement between the Peking Government and Russia, signed in that year, to operate in his territory. Thus does history repeat itself. Designs on the independence of Manchuria by Russia in the past were the reason actuating Chang in his determination to have no dealings with that country to-day. Even were there a new form of government in Moscow "friendly" to China, so far as Manchuria was concerned they had experienced Russian rule in the past, and were determined not to repeat the experiment, especially under the Soviet. Rather than agree to that, Manchuria formed a separate Government and prepared to defend its decision.

The move has special significance, since up to this moment Chang Tso Lin, once a Manchurian brigand, and now Dictator at Peking, defends his refusal to any compromise with the Southern Government, on the ground of its Bolshevik backing. He further reaffirmed the impossibility of relations with Russia, or, indeed, with any Government in alliance with that country.

The plan evolved in Chang Tso Lin's mind, of which a declaration of Manchurian independence was the first step, was not based on the reconquest of North and South. Chang was quite prepared to rest content with possession of Peking and its revenues, and for the time being, at all events, to allow the South to look after itself.

Difficulties confronted him in the carrying out of this plan, for, in addition to the Government of Dr. Yen, which controlled Peking, Chang had a rival in Wu Pei Fu, another provincial war lord who, operating from his own province of Honan, aimed at the unification of China, North and South, under his own leadership. Wu Pei Fu's power already extended over fourteen provinces, from Tsingtao across to Tibet, down the Yangtse and up to the northern frontier of China proper.

Thus Dr. Yen, who was styled "War Premier" in Peking, was faced with three rebellions simultaneously, of which the main one was the breakaway of almost all the country south of Canton, governed by the Kuomintang Republicans with the aid of Russian money and assistance. Next in importance came Wu Pei Fu's move to unite China by gaining possession of Peking and there forming a Government, backed by a strong army. Lastly, there was the shadow of returning Manchu power typified by Chang Tso Lin and his declaration of independence.

In Peking various Cabinets came and went during this final stage of the débâcle. In the majority of cases their lease of life was only a matter of weeks. Throughout 1925 the real power was divided between the two leaders, Tuan Chi Jui and Dr. Yen.

Chinese history gives numerous examples of two or three rebellions being less dangerous than one. In such circumstances rival jealousies usually operate in favour of the Government in power. The end of the Central Government of 1925, however, came through a combination of forces against Peking instead of, as in previous instances, another party coming to their aid.

Early in 1926 a coalition was evolved from the forces of Wu Pei Fu and Chang Tso Lin, the combined armies being sufficiently powerful to advance on Peking, rout the supporters of Tuan Chi Jui, and force the "President" of China to flee from the city.

On April 10, Chang Tso Lin and his ally were in full possession of the capital, forming what they described as an official Government of all China. Despite this declaration, and the fact that the Manchurian war lord still occupies the once Forbidden City, subsequent to that date there has been no real Government in China ; all semblance of authority has disappeared.

We now arrive at a point where, in order to have a clear view of the situation to-day, and the problem confronting European Powers, the narrative of 1926 must be taken in two parts. The first deals with events in the North since April, 1926, the second outlines their trend in the South, where the Cantonese Government claimed recognition as the national assembly. Aided and abetted by Soviet promises of material support and instruction, the South now entered upon the second stage of the interminable civil war.

Since April, 1926, the story of the North is mainly concerned with the efforts of four rival tuchuns, or provincial military governors, to agree among themselves, and furnish from their respective provinces the armies with which the Central Government at Peking could gain control over the South.

These war lords, who form the anti-Cantonese coalition, and upon whose forces the continuance of the Peking Government depends, are the celebrated Chang Tso Lin, the Manchurian leader ; Wu Pei Fu, ruling in Honan ; Sun Chuan-fang, the Governor of Kiangsu, part of Anhwei, and Chekiang ; and Chang Chung-chang, Governor of Shantung.

Chang Tso Lin, the best-known fighter of the North, has been in control of the Manchurian army since 1918. In those nine years he has survived many plots against his influence, including a mutiny of his own army, which he suppressed in a brilliant campaign.

After entering Peking with Wu Pei Fu in 1926, he encouraged the latter to open an immediate campaign against the Cantonese. It ended in the retreat of Wu Pei Fu, and left Chang Tso Lin in control of the greater part of Northern China, including Peking with its Central Government and revenues. At the moment of writing Chang Tso Lin is marching his armies south through Wu's territory, with a view to recapturing Hankow from the Cantonese, who secured possession of the Wohan cities and the middle Yangtse River last year, and have since made the combined cities of Hankow and Wuchang their capital.

Wu Pei Fu, Governor of Honan and supporter of the Central Government, has been styled the "gentleman of China." He is one of the most capable of the military governors who have afflicted the country with their personal squabbles since the overthrow of the monarchy, and was only defeated in his campaign against the Cantonese in 1926 by the treachery of subordinates. While an opponent of Bolshevism, he is critical of foreign rights in China, but since his defeat has lost prestige, and at present refuses active support to Chang Tso Lin in the campaign against the South.

Sun Chuan-fang, Governor of Kiangsu, was defeated by the Cantonese during their advance on Shanghai in February, 1927. He was born in that city forty-two years ago, and is a professional soldier of ability. In 1923 he was made Inspector-General of the South Central Provinces, and later, when Chang Tso Lin endeavoured to extend his control to Kiangsu, Sun Chuan-fang, concluding an alliance with Wu Pei Fu, drove off the Manchurian armies.

As a result of this he was invited to join hands with the Cantonese, but declined. The sequel came in the defeat of his army by the Southern forces, a reverse occasioned more by propaganda than by superior military tactics. Following the fall of Hangchow, the last important town on the road to Shanghai, Sun Chuan-fang was compelled to abandon his intention of playing

MARSHAL CHANG-TSO-LIN   GENERAL CHANG-KAI-SHEK

a "lone hand" and called in the Northern forces to defend the city. This last act of the defeated war lord led to the entry into Shanghai of the Shantung General, Chang Chung-chang, whose arrival to assume supreme command of its defence in place of Sun coincided with the landing of the British Defence Force sent to the Far East.

Marshal Chang Chung-chang is an imposing ex-brigand, six feet two inches in height, and when he occupied Shanghai on behalf of Chang Tso Lin in 1925 he and his fierce troops were decidedly unpopular. Upon his reappearance there in February, 1927, he declared that Bolshevism meant the disappearance of Chinese capital and property as well as foreign treaties, and stated that he and his Northern allies would make every effort to check the spread of this pernicious doctrine by the Cantonese.

An account of all the struggles, local fights, and bickerings of these Northern allies from April, 1926, until the moment when the danger to Shanghai galvanised them into action nine months later, would be endless, and only confuse the reader.

Passing over this period, therefore, and coming to the position on March 1, 1927, we find the allied armies of Chang Tso Lin and Wu Pei Fu controlling the provinces of Chihli, Shantung, Honan, Shansi, Hupeh, the three eastern provinces, and Manchuria. The Northern allies also claim authority over Hunan, Szechuan, and Shensi.

Nominally both these leaders, and also Chang Chung-chang, are subject to the orders of the phantom Central

Government at Peking, the Premier of which is now Liang Shi-Yi, a Chinese statesman well known in Great Britain. In practice, however, both Chang and Wu are more concerned with their own powers and respective shares of the Northern revenues than with those of the "shadow Government" they are supposed to be upholding against the Cantonese.

Owing to the constant regrouping of the various armies, due to desertions and the ceaseless propaganda, now a vital part of warfare in China, it is not possible to obtain exact figures of the military strength of the opposing forces.

After careful research I have compiled figures which are approximately correct. These show that the Northern alliance is still superior, both in numbers and equipment, to the Cantonese armies, and indicate that, given unity of command and honest leadership, there is no reason why Hankow, with the territory captured by the Cantonese forces during 1926, should not be restored to the North.

The strongest unit of the Northern force is Chang Tso Lin's army, numbering 150,000 men and 1,200 guns, and including a special brigade of "shock troops" recruited from "white" Russians who are refugees from that country. Behind this army, which garrisons Peking, are the arsenals in Manchuria, linked with the capital by a railway still in working order. Chang Tso Lin's troops should, therefore, be well equipped in arms and ammunition. Meanwhile their numbers may be increased by "press gang" methods during the southern operations.

Nor are Chang's forces so likely to be disaffected by agitators within their lines as other units of the Northern armies, for their leader is ruthless where insubordination is concerned, and swift death overtakes any man fomenting discontent.

Next in importance comes the army of Wu Pei Fu. It has been variously estimated at 250,000 upwards, but these figures cannot be accepted. A year ago the full extent of the " army " that could be relied upon to carry out his orders was approximately 10,000 men. Since then he has reorganised his forces, and built up a new reserve composed of recruits and deserters from elsewhere, who in China pass from one to another without even the formality of a change in uniform.

In January, 1927, Wu's army was 100,000 strong, but the news that Chang Tso Lin intended to march through his territory in a general advance against the South was followed by a mutiny instigated by Southern supporters in Wu's forces, and a large number of his men were disarmed to prevent their opening hostilities in support of the Cantonese.

Sun Chuan-fang originally commanded an army of 260,000 men, but his defeat outside Shanghai in January —largely due to a shortage of competent officers—and the constant desertions to the enemy has reduced the total to about 60,000. These troops are at present holding a front extending from Lake Tai-hu to the sea, where they intended to make a final stand, aided by forces brought up by Chang Chung-chang, the new defender of Shanghai, had the latter city not fallen.

A further contingent of 20,000 to 30,000 men was available for the defence of Nanking, since General Chang Chung-chang considered that the Cantonese would defer the attack on Shanghai pending the capture of that city. This would have cut the railway to Peking and isolated Shanghai. Included in the forces sent to hold Nanking was an armoured train and some "white" Russian advisers, but their movements are now uncertain.

Finally, the Northern forces include the remainder of the army under Chang Chung-chang, believed to total 150,000, making the combined armies at the nominal command of the Peking Government 450,000. Their resources in money and munitions are greater than those at the disposal of the Cantonese commanders, apart from Russian supplies, the extent of which is unknown. Up to the opening of the 1927 campaign, however, the morale of the Northern forces operating against the Cantonese—mostly troops of Sun Chuang-fang—was inferior to that of the South, while medical supplies and a hospital service are practically non-existent.

It is probable that the opening of a new and intensified campaign by Chang Tso Lin, and the reconstruction of Wu Pei Fu's forces, will see improvement, and the fighting of 1927 is likely to be noteworthy for a more bitter spirit on both sides, which will be evidenced in growing casualty lists. Under existing conditions of control the plan to win battles by agitation within the Northern lines will not carry the Southerners very far on the road to Peking. In the future the best fighting troops will gain the victories, apart from propaganda activities.

In a statement as to the probable course of the 1927 operations we must bear in mind a potential *rapprochement* between North and South on the basis of a united front to the foreigner. At present there is no sign of such unity eventuating. Indeed, the Northern leaders, despite rumours to the contrary, appear as strongly disinclined as ever to negotiate with a Government seeking to rule China by methods imported from Soviet Russia.

Such being the case, this year's campaign is likely to have for its main objects, so far as the North are concerned, the possession of Nanking and Shanghai and the recapture by Chang Tso Lin of Hankow and the towns lost on the Yangtse last year.

Whether the forces of the Central Government will be able to inflict such a decided check to the hitherto victorious Cantonese depends upon the strength, equipment, and morale of their opponents, concerning which I shall give some interesting facts later on in this chapter.

If the North can achieve their plan of campaign, or regain Nanking and Shanghai, their prestige will rise in proportion, and the claim of the Cantonese to recognition as the only possible Government of all China will suffer a rebuff from which they may never recover. The operations of 1927, therefore, bid fair to be the turning-point in the civil war.

I have narrated the determination of Chang Tso Lin and the Northern tuchuns to utilise their full financial and physical resources to hold Peking and control the revenues which, under the present financial arrangements, pass to some extent to those in possession of that city. Their attitude admitted of no compromise with a Cantonese Government under the influence of Moscow ; we will therefore consider the rival power of the South, which has already maintained the civil war for fifteen years, and with the proviso of Soviet aid might still continue to do so for an indefinite period.

The Kuomintang, or Cantonese party, whose rise is related in the previous chapter, ranks as the oldest and most efficient political organisation in China. It has a wide membership among Republicans and advanced Radicals, who have long aimed at eliminating the power of military organisations controlled by provincial governors. By a policy directed towards unification of a democratic China, and the withdrawal of rights enjoyed by foreigners, and freedom for the masses to organise into unions and strike when desired, the Cantonese have won much additional support, both from those Nationalists who wish to see foreign powers curtailed, and from the people in general who anticipate benefit by an extension of their rule.

The policy of the Kuomintang party is definitely progressive, and leadership is determined by party votes.

When formed by Sun Yat Sen and his executive in 1907, it was intended as an efficient organisation for Southern China, and a preparatory step to the reforms promised for 1912. Only after the revolution of 1911 was its full political aspect revealed.

Its strength to-day is approximately 750,000, but since the capture of Hankow and Shanghai, and the subtle efforts exerted to secure widespread support of the masses, its sympathisers probably total many millions.

The chief difficulty facing a separate Government in Canton in the initial stages was to raise funds for the pay and maintenance of the Southern troops. In China, more than in the West, hard cash dictates action, and the force whose pay is in arrear at once becomes subject to a process of disintegration.

The Kuomintang overcame this difficulty by two unprecedented steps. In defiance of the treaty rights enjoyed by foreign Powers, under which goods entering China shall not be taxed in excess of five per cent., they levied additional imposts of two and a half and five per cent. on all foreign imports to Canton, subsequently extending the levy to Hankow.

This step augmented their funds but did not, in the disturbed state of affairs, provide an amount adequate to meet their pressing demands. It was then that Moscow, foiled in its attempt to penetrate British India and foment discontent, offered monetary and material aid to the Cantonese forces, and so opened an avenue of escape to the Kuomintang leaders from their financial embarrassments.

The offer was accepted, although no data is available as to the sums ''lent'' by the Soviet to the Cantonese Government.

The Kuomintang now controlled two additional sources of wealth—surtaxes at the port of Canton and Russian loans. The financial aspect was further improved by the simple expedient of anticipating provincial taxes for 1928 and 1929, this original and drastic action being taken in the autumn of 1926.

The money thus raised supplied funds to sustain the

12

Cantonese advance against the three Northern war lords, Chang Tso Lin, Wu Pei Fu, and Sun Chuang-fang, the latter being the defender of Hangchow and Shanghai.

The first links between the Southern Government and the Soviet were forged shortly after the formation of a definite Government in Canton in 1918. From that date the initiative of the Kuomintang has in the main passed to Moscow.

A Soviet college was formed in Canton, "Red" agents were appointed from Moscow to proceed to Southern China and afford the requisite assistance to maintain the Cantonese party in power, and extend their influence throughout China. Groups of Chinese students travelled to Moscow to study the Soviet theory of government. So far as Southern China was concerned, from about 1920 its leaders had abandoned attempts to govern by methods suggested by, and suited to, the Chinese themselves, and actively prepared to put into practice Communist theories.

The Bolshevik domination in the Cantonese Government should not blind us to the fact that the Kuomintang party contains leaders of intellect and honesty of purpose.

Before dealing with further developments, there is an interesting and significant announcement emphasising the part played by the Soviet in the Chinese civil war and, more recently, in the agitation against all foreigners.

In a speech made at Moscow in December, 1926, Comrade Tan Peng Siang, of the Chinese section of the Communist International, declared :

" The real Chinese revolution began after the proletariat of Russia became the master of the country and was able to extend a helping hand to all oppressed nationalities. It is under the guidance and with the help of the Union of Socialist Soviet Republics that the Chinese revolution has undertaken to attain the following results : (1) To clear the country of all foreigners, (2) to repudiate all the agreements, (3) to make the Customs independent of foreigners, (4) to clear our waters of foreign vessels, (5) to return all foreign concessions to China, (6) to do away with all extra-territorial rights. All our victories are due to the help we have received from the Union of Socialist Soviet Republics, and it is with your help that we shall sweep all the imperialists into the sea."

The steps taken by European Powers to defend their legal rights against this policy of "Down with all foreigners" (presumably except Russians) will be dealt with in later chapters. What is of immediate interest is the effect of this policy on the Kuomintang itself.

For many months this party had been divided into Right and Left wings. Both moderates and extremists favour the abolition of foreign treaties and the return to China of concessions originally made to foreigners. That is the limit of their agreement.

The Right wing, comprising those leaders who believe that with the defeat of the North it will be feasible to dismiss their Russian advisers, are opposed to much of the Soviet activity in China, and advocate an early termination of the alliance.

The Left wing, led by Mr. Eugene Chen, favours continued alliance with Bolshevik Russia, with the support in material and personnel that it secures. Briefly, so far as concerns the attitude to foreigners, there is in the

Kuomintang party at the moment a Right wing favouring evolution, on the lines of the British Memorandum of December, 1926, and a Left wing demanding forcible expulsion of foreigners, and surrender of all " concessions " at present held by Great Britain and other Powers. The plan of campaign and method of organisation adopted by the extremists, who assumed the upper hand on the death of Sun Yat Sen in 1924, are based on the principles followed by the Bolsheviks after the Russian Revolution.

The Kuomintang, through Mr. Eugene Chen, declares that China has been ruined by war and revolution, by foreign oppression, and by foreign privileges and concessions extracted from corrupt Governments of the past who were not representative of the Chinese people.

So long as the Cantonese were the leaders of a local revolt similar to those that have often flared up in the past, to fade away again, leaving no appreciable change in the vast area of the Chinese Empire, such aims were of little consequence to the outside world. Up to 1924 a more or less established official Government existed in Peking, and all communications between Foreign Ministers and China were made to that Government. Even to-day the revenues derived from the Customs and the salt tax are paid to Chang Tso Lin, despite the Cantonese protest that their Government is alone entitled to rule in the name of the Chinese people.

When the Cantonese began their victorious northward thrust in 1926, and there loomed up the possible capture of Shanghai by the Southern Government, the question of a definite policy for the South became all-important.

This was dictated by several practical reasons, apart from the fact that Shanghai is the commercial nerve-centre of China, and one on which huge sums have been expended by Europeans in developing trade with China.

The intentions of the Cantonese Government, so far as they have been revealed, display a lack of constructive policy. They intend to drive out foreign traders, or at least to dictate terms and taxes governing foreign commerce. They have made attractive promises to Chinese workers throwing in their lot with the revolution, and thus facilitated the work of their own armies by fomenting strikes behind the lines held by the troops of the North. There is, however, no indication of any sound constructive policy promising peace and prosperity to China in the future. They apparently believe that with the capture of Peking, and expulsion of the foreigner, the future will be assured.

As in Russia, the workers are the basis of the Cantonese movement. They are seeking to organise the "mighty masses" of China, and to form a Labour Army, which, by fighting, strikes, or propaganda—the form to be adopted is immaterial; in fact, all three weapons are being used—will enforce Cantonese rule over China proper. For the first time the country will have been conquered, not by a foreign dynasty, or by the bayonets of mercenaries, but by the Chinese people themselves, who will henceforth form the Government and give the national effort full scope in shaping the future.

It is doubtful if this programme can be put into practice, for a study of Chinese history shows that the

continuity of the family system of social life for forty
centuries has produced few leaders. Setting that, however, aside, a complete transformation of the Chinese
people would have to be effected and the ingrained precepts and principles handed down from time immemorial
must go by the board. Such sweeping changes are not
accomplished overnight.

What the present experiment may lead to in the future
cannot be foreseen, but it is all too probable that the
triumph of the Cantonese Government, with its basic
power derived from a people ninety-seven per cent. of
whom are illiterate, will be followed by a breakdown of
the attempt at democratic government and the rise of
some new dictator.

So far this question has not arisen, and whilst
"government" means for Canton the waging of war
on Peking and the foreign elements, it is comparatively easy for the Cantonese to gain support
from the masses by a promise of power. For these
reasons the formation of labour unions has been
encouraged, and in Southern China there are now 280
separate unions with political bureaus controlled by Soviet
agents.

I have reverted to the Soviet influence in the Cantonese
Government since at the moment it is predominant,
and in the event of victory for the Cantonese forces it
would be quickly revealed that the present revolution is,
neither in its inspiration nor direction, truly national, but
directed mainly from Moscow.

China to-day has, I believe, a brilliant opportunity of
forming a national Government based on the rule of the

people, if only the Right wing of the Kuomintang party can gain control of the machine and produce leaders of genuine capacity.

An immense task awaits whoever wishes to establish settled rule. An entirely new standard of thought, a public spirit, and the subordination of personal to national gain, the elimination of bribery and corruption, and the substitution of healthy ideas for the loose moral and political standard that has characterised Chinese polity since the days long before the Christian era, must be brought in. It took Europe several centuries to effect its own transformation. Can the Chinese, under past and present circumstances, accomplish the same within a generation? He who anticipates that would indeed be sanguine.

Opportunity is a great thing. It was probably due to the failure of the Soviet in its attempt to stir up trouble in the East that caused Moscow to see in the formation of a separate Government in South China the chance to strike a telling blow at Great Britain and other nations through China.

I shall discuss the real nature of Russian Soviet aims, as distinct from those of the Chinese leaders, in a subsequent chapter. Before dealing with this aspect of the problem, and the concessions and foreign trade, it is well to outline certain facts relative to the diplomatic and armed forces with which the Cantonese party have progressed to date.

Careful estimates by expert observers on the spot estimate the strength of the Cantonese army in April, 1927, at 200,000 men, or 300,000 if nondescripts and new recruits are counted.

This force, which has had the dual task of holding Hankow and the Wuhan cities against the Northerners, and capturing Shanghai and Nanking, is the best armed and equipped in China. It numbers in its ranks many Russian, and Russian-trained, officers and advisers, and the Moscow authorities attach sufficient importance to a Cantonese victory to pour further trainloads of guns and munitions into Southern China, if development in the 1927 campaign demands further assistance to ensure victory for the Kuomintang.

The armies are equipped with modern rifles, hand grenades, and light artillery, and have aeroplanes and siege-guns—the latter not at the disposal of their opponents. They have, moreover, the active assistance of entire corps of Chinese and Russian propagandists, organised by Jacob Borodin, the Russian "dictator" at Hankow, whose rôle is to lighten the task of the army by fomenting strikes and mutinies within the Northern lines. It will be remembered that the rising of the working masses against foreigners and the Central Government preceded the capture of Hankow in 1926, a similar outbreak occurring at Shanghai in February, when it seemed that the capture of the latter city was imminent.

The bulk of the Southern forces have had little experience of war, and are inferior to the Northern, but their inexperience is counterbalanced by the fervour which their leaders have aroused for the "crusade" to liberate China from both war lords and foreigners, with the added promise to introduce a Soviet system of government which, as I have shown, would for the first time give real power to the masses.

From left to right: Michael Borodin, Russian Adviser to the Kuomintang; Kuo-Ming-yu, Head of Kuomintang Propaganda; Mrs. Borodin; Mrs. Lioo Chung-kai; Mrs. Chiang Kai-shek; General Gallent, Russian Military Adviser; and (seated) Chiang Kai-shek, beside whom is his son

The Commander-in-Chief of the Cantonese army is Chiang Kai-Shek, who first became prominent in 1924, when he was appointed head of the Whampoa Cadet School, where, with the assistance of Russian experts, he trained officers for the Southern army. Later he took the field against the Yunnan and Kwangsi forces, both of which he defeated, thus making himself a national figure. Continuing his campaign, he won over Tang Sheng-chih, formerly Military Governor of South Honan, and defeated Wu Pei Fu, and so gained control of the middle Yangtse, with the important trading towns of Hankow and Kuikiang.

Collaborating with him in these victories is a mystery figure—General Gallents, a former Austrian staff officer, who, after 1918, served first with the Bolshevik army, and later went to China to assist the Cantonese forces.

Allied to these two Generals, although as yet taking little part in the campaign, is Feng Yu-hsiang, the best-known war lord who has hitherto joined the Cantonese. Feng is the " Christian " General who taught his troops to sing hymns on the march, and after his defeat by the combined forces of Wu Pei Fu and Chang Tso Lin in 1925 resigned his command and proceeded to Moscow. There he studied Soviet methods, returning in the autumn of 1926 to assume control of part of Wu Pei Fu's forces that had gone over to the Cantonese. Feng has since joined in the anti-British propaganda issued from Canton, but it is doubtful whether his forces at the moment number more than 30,000 men, so that the support which he can offer to the Cantonese commanders is limited.

So far as numbers are concerned the Cantonese can muster only about 250,000 troops, against a strength of 450,000 at the disposal of their opponents. Owing to the necessity of defending Hankow, part of the Southern army was prevented from taking part in the capture of Shanghai.

There are, however, two factors in the confused situation favouring the Cantonese hopes. Their troops are, thanks to Russian assistance, better armed, equipped, and led than the forces opposed to them, whilst the steady tide of propaganda flowing ahead is an additional and powerful asset. Appeals to " national " sentiment against the foreigner and the military governor have always been a popular cry in China, and by encouraging the working classes to organise their unions, and to use their new strength for the enforcement of better working conditions, regardless of the ability of employers to meet these demands, have caused thousands of illiterate coolies to hail the Cantonese Government as saviours.

In China battles have often been won by money than with more orthodox weapons. Many contests in her history have been avoided at the eleventh hour by the sudden decision of some military governor to transfer his allegiance, and his forces, to the other side. The Cantonese, therefore, count on the power of money and propaganda as the decisive factors in defeating the coalition against them.

At the moment money is lacking, but with the capture of Shanghai, they may become masters of the rich Customs revenue collected from foreign traders at that port.

Upon their ability to replenish the war-chest rests to a considerable extent the fate of their Government and the chances of ultimate victory. With Shanghai, Canton, and Hankow securely in their power, and the tariffs at these ports enhanced from five per cent. to ten per cent., they will hold the requisite cash for further munitions and to buy over any opponent susceptible to bribery.

If the Cantonese can hold Shanghai, with its revenues, and large Chinese population as a potential reinforcement to their army, they will be in a favourable position for a general advance on Peking in the near future.

The next few months will decide whether the Cantonese forces are near to final success. Assuming that the armies of the allied war lords of the North hold together, the campaign of 1927 may see the Southern troops retreating from Hankow rather than their collectors demanding control of the Customs revenues of Shanghai from the British advisers who now control them on behalf of the Central Government at Peking.

EXTRA-TERRITORIALITY AND CUSTOMS

CHAPTER VIII

EXTRA-TERRITORIALITY AND CUSTOMS

In the crisis between China and the foreign Powers there are three distinct issues, of which the one dealing with concessions has been treated in a previous chapter, so that we will now discuss that of extra-territoriality—the crux of the problem—and the Maritime Customs.

The cumbersome title of extra-territoriality is the right exercised by the British Government, through its consular and judicial authorities in China, over British subjects who are beyond the jurisdiction of the laws of China, and can only be dealt with for any offence by those authorities. The necessity for this has been evidenced in previous chapters, and it is clear that the laws and judicial system of China are in such a lamentable state that European and American Powers have not felt themselves justified in confiding their nationals to the care of Chinese law.

The right that foreign subjects should be amenable to their own laws dates back to 1620, when the Treaty of Nerchinsk between Russia and China was signed. This, and subsequent agreements, contained clauses relating to extra-territoriality, and in those concluded by ourselves at different periods the privilege was, as far as possible, limited to meeting the demands imposed by trade and commerce, with due regard to Chinese sovereignty and non-interference with their legal and social institutions.

The last Power to obtain these rights was Japan at the close of the Chino-Japanese War of 1894-95.

The Treaty of Nanking, signed in 1842, made provision for consular officers at the five ports opened, and by general regulations drafted a year later definite arrangements were concluded for British law to apply to our own nationals.

Before discussing the various phases of extra-territoriality, a brief review of the Chinese laws and how they arose will be of interest, for it has been truly said that these form a fascinating study in the history of any country. This applies with particular force to China, essentially the land of old customs that has evolved rules and regulations of remarkable antiquity and interest.

They were formulated from the dictates and writings of the sages, who have played the dominant part in the social life of the nation, the maxims laid down having been evolved through the ages, and of a nature applicable to an empire that had no parallel in the world's history. The system of law thus devised, although adapted to the genius of the Chinese people, embodied sentences and punishments totally at variance with Western ideas. In its application it might be characterised as a travesty of justice, for, *inter alia,* it took no account of truthful evidence and of that of competent eyewitnesses. The solicitude shown to the prisoner, and the accepted canon that a man is innocent until he is proved guilty, were beyond the comprehension of Chinese jurists. As the famous Sir Robert Hart once remarked, everything in China is anomalous, and everything has the atmosphere of antiquity. So it is with the law, the first promulgation of which took place as far back as 2357 B.C., although from the records of that time there appears to have been slight need for any legal machinery, the rule of the existing dynasty being regarded as the ideal example of government.

As each successive dynasty came on the Celestial stage so the law underwent enlargement or modification, the same general principles being adhered to, regard only being paid to changing conditions, and the necessity of adopting enactments more suited to cope with them. In time the laws were codified, and reduced to writing for circulation amongst the provinces, the earliest known examples, about six centuries before the Christian era, being engraved on metal tablets.

Under such constantly varying conditions, and with the peculiar standard of life of the Chinese people, it is not to be expected that they could equal the principles evolved in Europe after centuries of application, but as a legal system adapted to the Chinese race, and bearing in mind the great difference in variety and bearing of the population, it was eminently suited to its own particular requirements.

In a previous chapter I have shown that the basis of government was centred on the family and parental authority, this being the force holding the Chinese people together, and for the successful conduct of which the law was regulated.

As regards its application, it has many drawbacks, of which I shall deal with some of the most vital, and those that impressed me as a Consul-General and a Judge.

Detention of accused and others in the yamens, or magisterial headquarters, is an objectionable feature of the Chinese system. This is frequently the case pending an investigation ; it opens up a wide field to gaolers and others who exploit the opportunities thus afforded of extracting illegal commissions. Persons so detained languish in prison awaiting trial or investigation in proportion to the amount they can produce to satisfy the demands of the prison staff.

That this is no uncommon occurrence was evidenced in a recent case in which two accused had been in prison for over two years ; they possessed little beyond what they stood up in, their property had been attached by the court to meet the claims of extortionate money-lenders, but no actual charge was ever laid against the accused themselves, and so I was successful in securing their release by the local magistrate.

Often prejudice is shown against the prisoner, little regard is paid to points that may tell in his favour, and a confession is insisted upon before punishment is awarded. This leads to every kind of abuse, and provincial officials adopt various means for enforcing confession, while they can reduce the state of mind of the accused person to a point where he will do and act as directed. In the western provinces, for example, it is no uncommon thing for a prisoner to be kept awake for days on end in order that his mind may be brought to such a condition that he is ready to do and say whatever is demanded of him. This is the work of a gaoler who by judicious prods at intervals, when the unfortunate man gives way to sleep, keeps him awake until, like the hawk when it undergoes training is deprived of sleep in order to render it docile and obedient, he becomes amenable to the dictates of those controlling his destiny and the case in which he is involved. It is both subtle and effective, for there is no bodily evidence that the man has undergone this form of torture.

There are, of course, exceptions to the general rule, and we find Chinese magistrates honestly desirous of probing the depths of a case and arriving at a fair verdict. I have already commented on the perspicacity and clear-sightedness of the Celestial race and their practical mind. The Chinese official is by no means hidebound, nor does he rely solely upon precedent or immemorial custom as the solution of a difficulty. He is distinctly a man of resource, and endeavours by other means to attain the desired end. One magistrate showed his acumen in detection of a robbery case that came up for trial at his court. Four men were involved in the affair, but the evidence was conflicting, and the case was therefore adjourned until the morrow. When the court re-assembled the magistrate took out the four accused to a temple hard by, closed the doors, and then made them kneel down by the wall which had previously been covered with lampblack. The building was in darkness, and he directed them to place their hands upon the wall and pray, adding that whoever had committed the crime would have a black mark upon his forehead. The simple tiller of the soil amongst the four, who was really the culprit, became alarmed, and quietly endeavoured to efface the mark that he imagined must be on his forehead, with the result that when the door was flung open and the light poured in, the thief was revealed in all his blackness.

As regards legal reform and the codification of the laws, this should be the work of the immediate future ; it was, in fact, initiated with the formation of a Law Codification Commission in 1904. Their labours up to 1922 had resulted in the preparation of five codes, with the help of foreign legal experts, and based on modern jurisprudence. Further, a system of law courts was introduced in 1910, the judges attached to them being trained on modern lines, and not eligible for appointment unless in possession of certain qualifications. This is all to the good, but we must remember that they apply only to those provinces in the vicinity of Peking and the large cities ; beyond the zone of central government matters are still medieval, for to the central and western provincial magistrate, and those in the region of Burmah, India, and Central Asia, Peking is remote, and its influence is exhausted long before it reaches those areas.

In response to Chinese objections that the existence of extra-territorial rights was an infringement of their sovereignty, an agreement was concluded between Great Britain and China in 1902, under which it was stipulated that China, desirous of reforming her judicial system and bringing it into line with that of Western nations, should receive assistance from Great Britain to that end, who, when satisfied that the state of Chinese law and the arrangements for its application warranted her in so doing, should surrender existing privileges.

In 1903 a similar agreement was entered into with the

United States, and it is of sufficient importance to quote Article 15 of that document. "Reformation of judicial system. Extra-territoriality to terminate. The Government of China having expressed a strong desire to reform its judicial system and to bring it in accord with that of Western nations, the United States agrees to relinquish extra-territorial rights when satisfied that the state of Chinese laws, the arrangements for their administration, and other conditions warrant it in so doing."

A clause to that effect was also inserted in the agreement concluded with Japan in 1903.

At the Washington Conference convened in 1921 the matter was definitely raised by the Chinese delegation, and their case was in the main presented by Dr. Wang, who, in his address, admitted that the principles of extra-territorialty had been clearly laid down in various treaties concluded with the Powers. The main plank in his argument for abolition of the rights was that when they were originally granted there were but five treaty ports open to the world ; there were now about fifty such trading centres with a greatly increased number of foreigners resident in, and visiting, the ports, and commercial points over whom the Chinese had no jurisdiction. The anomaly, he argued, brought foreigners into incessant conflict with local authority and administration, and in general it impaired their territorial integrity.

The British and American Governments were desirous of giving every assistance to China that she might preserve her juridical integrity. But however sympathetic they might be, the question was obviously one of fact rather than of principle, existing conditions had to be borne in mind, and it was only just to carry out an impartial investigation as to the administration of Chinese law since the agreements already alluded to. It was essential to obtain a clear and definite idea as to present conditions ; indeed, Dr. Wang did not ask for an immediate relinquishment of the rights, but requested that a definite date might be fixed.

The Conference in pursuance of its desire to bring about a satisfactory solution, appointed a Commission to inquire into the judicial system and the question of extra-territoriality in general, but no authority was given to conclude an agreement. It comprised delegates from Great Britain, United States, France, Italy, Spain, Japan, Norway, Belgium, the Netherlands, Sweden, Denmark, and Portugal. China was represented by one of its most able lawyers.

The Commission was to commence its work in 1925, but owing to the fighting and civil warfare raging throughout all the provinces adjacent to Peking and Shanghai, its task did not begin before January, 1926. It held altogether twenty-one meetings, and the committee appointed to investigate local conditions, prisons, courts, and magisterial areas carried out a wide programme of travel. Owing to the vast distances involved the investigations of the committee were necessarily confined to provinces adjacent to the large cities. It is significant that the Cantonese declined to receive the travelling committee, or to assist the commission in any way, arguing that the extra-territorial rights should be abrogated without investigation. It would have been well for the committee to see prison conditions in the south as an additional argument in favour of retaining the rights until reform has been really instituted and carried out.

The work of this Commission is of vital importance, and I therefore quote from its report and the conclusions at which it arrived. Dealing with the main point at issue, it says : " One of the chief factors which militates against the normal administration of justice in China to-day is the interference with the departments of civil government by the military leaders. The military interference with the civil administration extends to the judiciary, so that the independence of this branch of the Government is endangered. Irregularities in this respect usually occur under the guise of the application of martial law, which, however, is declared without regard to legal provisions on the subject. Another important factor is the control by the military of the finances of the Government, so that the courts are dependent upon the military for their financial support. By virtue of Chinese law itself the legal position of the military renders them immune from the jurisdiction of the ordinary courts, while their power, in fact, often renders them immune from all courts. This immunity is liable to be extended to the friends of the military, and to the commercial firms and organisations in which they are interested. Ample evidence of the foregoing is brought out by the fact that the military are constantly committing crimes which go unpunished, for it is generally difficult for aggrieved civilians to obtain any redress from military authorities commanding their own armies, when such redress must be sought in military courts controlled by these authorities. The callous attitude of the military with respect to the situation thus described is emphasised by the fact that since the Extra-Territorial Commission has been sitting in Peking, or shortly prior thereto, there have been notable instances of executions and other acts perpetrated by them, both in the city of Peking itself and in the provinces, in such complete disregard of the principles of justice that the Commission would neglect its duty if it did not refer to them.''

The law as applied in China is also discussed, the conduct of the police and their high-handedness and corruption are dealt with, whilst it is placed on record that '' cases of torture for the purpose of extracting confessions of guilt, and for the punishment of certain offences, as well as cases of ill-treatment of prisoners, still occur in China. It is only fair to state, however, that the instances of torture and maltreatment that have come to the attention of the Commission have been perpetrated by the military, the magistrates, and the police. In regard to the modern courts, no such instances have been reported.''

It is significant that no facilities were afforded the Commission to see the workings of any of the police tribunals, and it had reluctantly to arrive at the conclusion, after certain facts, that the administration of justice there was unsatisfactory. It cannot be said that the Commission was assisted in its labours ; obstruction there undoubtedly was, as will always be the case where there are defects to conceal, and it is not desired that too much should be seen. In this connection no opportunity was given to inspect any of the old style district prisons, police gaols, or military prisons, whilst the Commissioners animadvert strongly on the habit of the local police in arresting small children for minor offences and contravention of the law.

I have myself visited some old style prisons which still flourish in all their terror. They are within the magisterial yamen, and once inside realism can be studied with effect. One that I visited contained prisoners who were lodged in dark rooms with only an opening in the ceiling eighteen inches square for light and ventilation. The floor reeked with the dirt and filth of years, and as I groped my way in the semi-darkness I stumbled over the prostrate form of a man chained to a stake in the ground. Striking a match I beheld a creature dirty and begrimed, in the last stages of degradation, confined in a hole worse than a kennel. Others were chained together to a board secured by stakes in the floor of this black hole. No tendance of any kind was given the prisoners, the State having a distinctly limited interest in the welfare of those committed to gaol.

In the west, too, some of the punishments are ingenious and cruel, being awarded according to the nature of the crime. For serious offences, which we might term manslaughter, the criminal may be placed in a cage with his head through an opening at the top. He stands on layers of bricks which are just high enough to support him without strain on the head. These are gradually removed, one every day, until his toes barely touch the ground, and he is thus left to die by slow strangulation.

To enforce a confession, to which I have previously

alluded, the man will be made to kneel on broken crockery or thinly spread maize, a painful performance which is not readily apparent.

Having fulfilled its task the Commission made certain recommendations, being of the opinion that when they shall have been reasonably complied with the several Powers would be warranted in relinquishing their respective rights of extra-territoriality. It now only remains for the Chinese themselves to institute such measures as shall rapidly contribute to that end.

Much has already been accomplished in the past ten years in the compilation of new laws, and the promulgation of codes and regulations devised to bring about an improved state of affairs, but the interminable civil war, and the fact that there is neither in the north or south any representative body that can really speak for the Chinese people stultifies hope of immediate reform.

Another question raised at the Washington Conference, and forming a subject of dispute in the present crisis, was the vexed problem of tariffs and customs which had been limited by former treaties. By an agreement concluded there it was arranged that a Commission should endeavour to abolish *likin* and other dues, and levy such surtaxes upon imports as it might consider advisable, and it was to meet in China at a time and place indicated by the Chinese Government. Unfortunately, owing to the same causes that have held up the abolition of extra-territoriality, no progress has been made. The Commission met after many difficulties incidental to the fighting and the railways being held by predatory bands, Great Britain, United States, France,

MOUNTAIN TORRENT OF THE UPPER YANGTSE RIVER, NEAR ITS
SOURCE IN THE KUEN LUN MOUNTAINS OF TIBET

IN THE YANGTSE VALLEY

Italy, Japan, and eight other smaller Powers being represented. China had ten Commissioners, so that her
interests were, at any rate, well catered for.

The Chinese delegates suffered from the vagaries of
strife and politics ; they were deputed by the various
sides, and as the fortunes of war went this way or that,
so were they compelled to conform, and to seek refuge
in a foreign concession as rivals came into power. Indeed,
so chaotic was the state of affairs, and so precarious the
existence of these delegates, that on April 10, 1926,
when Chang Tso Lin effected his *coup d'état,* and the
President was compelled to hurriedly quit Peking, there
were only three left with which to resume the work of
this harassed conference. Despite the difficulties that
were constantly arising, and the obstacles placed in the
way of a satisfactory adjustment of tariffs, the foreign
delegates made great efforts to give effect to the
Washington resolution, and the surtaxes provided for in
the agreement, as well as to negotiate forthwith a
fresh treaty with a view to bringing in all the revenue
that trade could produce. Civil war and chaos had
their way ; Peking was a whirlpool of plot, intrigue,
and outrage, Chinese delegates came and went, the
foreign members carried on in the hope of framing a
tariff schedule which would give China the opportunity
to put her house in order and begin the work of reconstruction. All to no purpose, however. There is little hope
of the Commission being able to bring the good work to
fruition in the near future.

Under existing conditions the levy of unauthorised
taxation proceeds apace, whilst both North and South

are now engaged on the collection of surtaxes. Before going into this matter I will deal with the more or less authorised taxation, of which the *likin,* an impost on merchandise in transit from one province to another, fixed originally at one-tenth of one per cent., is an important one. It has caused much trouble and inconvenience to Chinese and foreigners alike, for the arbitrary and capricious way in which it is levied brings the traders into conflict with the authorities.

The *likin* is an interesting feature of Chinese history, being voluntarily levied, as already explained, by the people during the Taiping Rebellion of 1863 for provision of funds to meet expenses imposed by that outbreak. It was primarily intended to supplement the land tax, being confined to sales, and the money thus raised was to be devoted to the military object specified. It was regarded only as a temporary measure, and was later extended to cover goods in transit in the interior. The looseness of its organisation naturally gave rise to the usual abuses ; the amounts collected varied in the different provinces, tolls were set up along the main trade routes and on the waterways, and the sums collected varied in accordance with the rapacity or otherwise of the local officials. The tax soon became a serious obstacle to trade and commerce, and, not being recognised by treaty, has always been objected to by foreign Powers. Despite the assurance given at the time, and on subsequent occasions, that the tax would be discontinued so soon as the finances of the country were in a satisfactory condition, this has never been redeemed, and there is less likelihood of its abolition, for the need of the warring sides for money becomes more acute as time goes on.

Unfortunately we have in the past given tacit recognition to the *likin,* and it is therefore difficult to secure its abolition unless a compromise can be reached. Since it has no definite character and no regularity in its incidence, the continuance of such a tax is a serious menace to trade. It is never possible to give figures where Chinese administration is concerned, but prior to the advent of the Republic it was estimated that of the amount collected provincially on the *likin* barely 12 per cent. passed into the State coffers, so much being appropriated on the way. Then there is always the want of confidence in one another, each province is profoundly suspicious of its neighbour; the Central Government is looked upon with even greater mistrust, and there is a constant warfare of deceit and misrepresentation as to income and expenditure.

Efforts have been made to secure uniformity for foreigners in the *likin,* and the treaties stipulate that foreign merchants in import and export commerce should pay to the Maritime Customs $7\frac{1}{2}$ per cent. instead of the usual 5 per cent., to be then exempt from the *likin;* but in practice this has never been followed.

This brings us to consideration of the Imperial Maritime Customs, the most important institution in China and the one stable department of government that stands out pre-eminently from the welter of anarchy and disruption, and is a remarkable example of what can be accomplished by honest administration. It was formed in an original way. Owing to the capture of Shanghai by the Taiping rebels in 1853, affairs became so disorganised that the Chinese official on the spot, who had hitherto collected the dues for his Government, found himself unable to do so, and appealed to the Consuls of Great Britain, the United States, and France for assistance, and as a result a representative from each nation was detailed to assist in the formation of a Customs administration. The system worked so well that the Chinese requested that it might be applied to the remaining treaty ports, and this was followed by the appointment of an Inspector-General in the person of Mr. H. N. Lay, who was later succeeded by Mr. Hart, afterwards the famous Sir Robert Hart. The latter assumed control in 1863, and during his period of upwards of fifty years in China he brought the Imperial Maritime Customs to a high state of efficiency.

In accordance with an agreement between the two Governments, it was arranged that the Inspector-General should be a British subject so long as our trade predominates in China.

When first organised, the Peking Government disposed of the proceeds in the proportion of two-fifths to the Imperial Treasury and three-fifths to the Provinces. After the Chino-Japanese War in 1894, and the collapse of the Manchu régime, various foreign loans, dealt with in previous chapters, had been negotiated and the liabilities thus incurred were guaranteed by the Maritime Customs, the balance after satisfaction of the loan charges being handed to the Central Government.

It is not only with regard to foreign and domestic debt that the Customs has been the saving grace ; it covers a far wider field, for the regulations deal with the conduct of foreign trade, levy of various duties and their collection, whilst it is also engaged in harbour control, conservancy, and lighting of the coasts, which are dangerous and needed to be well provided for in that respect.

The duties are performed with the greatest efficiency and to the benefit of all concerned, more particularly to China, and it would be fatal to allow any irresponsible interference with its working at the present juncture.

In 1863 the amount collected by the Maritime Customs was approximately two million pounds sterling ; since that date the increase has been marked year by year, as trade grew under assurance of stable conditions and removal of the shadow of illegal ˙imposition, until in 1926 it had totalled the sum of 78,100,000 taels, of which 33,000,000 taels were collected in Shanghai, an increase of 6,250,000 taels over 1925. (1 tael equalled 3s. $1\frac{3}{8}$d.)

The amount levied on all imports and exports passing through the treaty ports is a flat rate of 5 per cent. on all articles, with a few minor exceptions, which the Treaty Powers are willing to increase to $7\frac{1}{2}$ per cent. or more. In view of the Chinese statements of higher rates imposed on Chinese goods entering certain foreign countries, it should be taken into account that, whilst some of those duties may be high, on a large number of articles it is nil ; China, on the other hand, has the flat rate on practically everything imported or exported, and therefore gains in the aggregate.

Intimately connected with taxation as at present exploited is the opium question.

China and opium have always been closely associated, but of recent years stringent laws were drafted and wholehearted attempts made by the Chinese Government to eradicate the evil. In 1917 they had practically succeeded when the cumulative effect of civil war and internecine strife rendered those efforts abortive. The warring sides saw their sources of income diminishing, the wherewithal to pay their following became increasingly scarce ; new ways and means must be discovered, fresh sources tapped, and so it came to pass that opium and its cultivation and preparation offered a sure and ready solution to the financial straits in which all alike were involved.

The new state of affairs was not only due to the latter cause ; it was in the main accounted for by the inability of the Central Government to exercise control over the provinces and officials, both civil and military, who encouraged, and, in many cases, forced the people to cultivate the poppy. Further, the numerous war lords created monopolies in the traffic in flagrant defiance of the law, for which they have no regard.

The effect of this recrudescence of a vicious habit, with all the baneful consequences that follow in its wake, was felt not only in China ; it penetrated beyond, and has done much to swell the illicit traffic in the drug in all parts of the world. To such an extent has it progressed since the civil war assumed widespread and far-reaching proportions, that expert authority on the spot and those engaged in the closest investigation are unable to give even an approximate estimate of the amount produced in China in the past five years. The Opium Commission of the League of Nations endeavoured to ascertain the facts from the Chinese Government, but the results were unsatisfactory, and with the passing of law and order it is no longer possible to gauge the truth.

In the provinces of Yunnan, Fukien, Hupeh, Anhwei, Kansu, Shensi, Szechuan, and Kiangsu reports show that although regulations have been issued nominally prohibiting cultivation, with heavy penalties to the poppy grower, they have long been a dead letter. Indeed, official recognition is now general, and in some cases the pay of the troops is in the form of opium. As the war lord's position is dependent upon his army, and a mutiny at once occurs when pay is in arrear, no consideration can interfere with the necessity of exploiting such a source of profit.

As regards India, an understanding with China was arrived at in 1907 restricting import of Indian opium to ten per cent. for a period of three years, the Chinese to reduce production of the native article in the same proportion. In 1911, by agreement, the export of Indian opium to China and the production of the drug in China itself were to cease by 1917. Cultivation in, and export from, India to China had for many years been a source of revenue to the Indian Government ; the war between Great Britain and China in 1840 being partly attributable to this traffic. The agreement of 1911 further provided that opium should not be taken into any Chinese province that could prove that the production of native opium had ceased. This was one of the steps taken by the Chinese to eradicate the evil, and the

14

traffic was well within control when it received the set-back already referred to.

With a strong demand for a prohibited article the means to meet it are not difficult to create, especially in a land where dominion and authority are but shadowy and corruption is rife. My own position regarding the opium traffic was, in common with other matters, of political import, ill-defined, and often equivocal, and in the absence of definite instructions I had to steer a middle course. Moreover, in the past the situation was anomalous from the fact that practically all the foreign opium imported into China originated in India, although the bulk of it was consumed in the coast provinces. The Chinese were grateful for the Indian prohibition, but were dubious as to its effect, since no restriction was placed on the sale of the drug to markets whence it could be passed into China. This is the basic principle on which the Chinese argument is pivoted whenever a case of opium smuggling comes up for disposal in which the Indian article or Indian subjects are involved.

In January, 1913, the Indian Government announced that it would ban the export of opium to China, and the last sale of opium at Calcutta for export to China took place in April of that year. A net annual revenue of £3,000,000 was thus voluntarily relinquished by this act.

The disposal of the opium stocks at Hong Kong and the treaty ports of China was then proceeded with. In 1914 they totalled approximately 10,000 chests ; these were gradually reduced, but the opium commanded enormous prices. The temptation was great, and after some hesitation action was taken which cast suspicion on the sincerity of the Chinese Government. Rumours of schemes, in which high Chinese officials were interested, for the purchase of the opium and its sale to the public began to circulate. For three years public opinion, Chinese and foreign, was able to prevent the schemes from materialising, but in 1918 the 1,200 chests remaining were actually purchased by the Government, a transaction that was widely condemned, protests being lodged by the British and American Ministers, and Mr. Hsu Shih-chang, then President of the Republic, ordered the opium to be destroyed.

Apart from this, there were other sinister influences at work; stocks were purchased and held by wealthy Chinese when it was realised that prohibition was really intended, whilst the ban gave rise to much smuggling from Siberia, where cultivation is practicable, from the Portuguese settlement of Macao near Canton, and other places in the East to which Indian opium was still exported.

The responsibility of Great Britain and India for the use of opium in China has been greatly and consistently exaggerated. A trade in the drug there existed long before the Portuguese doubled the Cape of Good Hope, and they were the first Europeans to open up the traffic. From the Red Sea and the Persian Gulf it was conducted by the Arabs, the opium carried being Turkish, Indian, and possibly Persian.

It is not generally known that for many years prior to our advent opium was on the Chinese Customs tariff at Canton, being admitted as a medicine on payment of duty, but there is evidence that it was regarded as contraband as early as 1764. From Chinese records, however, it was contraband merely because it was not included among the articles in which foreign commerce was allowed.

Further, the Chinese records show that the seeds of the poppy were used for medicinal purposes as early as A.D. 973, and there is a reference to opium in the work of Wang Hsi, who died in 1488.

The suppression of the opium traffic is still engaging the serious attention of the League of Nations, most of the States who are parties to the League assisting at the conferences. The Russian Soviet, however, declined the invitation to attend, and gave vent to derisive statements implying bad faith to the nations participating, and asserted that the latter are merely endeavouring to serve their own commercial interests and gain material benefit.

These remarks were singularly inopportune, for at the time the poppy was being cultivated and the drug prepared in Asiatic Russia. The Province of Semirechinsk, in Russian Turkistan, is the chief opium growing centre, and during the summer the districts adjacent to Tokmak and the Issik Lake, where the soil is adapted to the growing of the poppy, are active in the preparation of the drug, which may eventually find its way to the opium dens of Limehouse and the secret orgies that occasionally come to light in the West End.

The existence of this opium traffic, which has escaped notice, makes possible not only Soviet taxation, but an extensive system of exchange. Large quantities of manufactured goods, raw and prepared leather, cloth goods, and material of everyday use were imported into

Russia from Chinese territory in exchange for opium, and often the drug was paid for when taken over in Semire-chinsk with the cotton cloth of Chinese Turkistan, home-made boots, and Manchester chintzes and muslins. These last are brought through India and over the Karakoram Mountains, the world's highest trade route, on which seven passes must be crossed, the lowest being 16,000 feet and the highest 18,300 feet. It is curious to think that the produce of the Lancashire mills should be the medium of exchange for a drug that affects directly and indirectly half the population of Asia.

A considerable amount of opium is grown in Afghanistan, whence it is imported into China through the Afghan province of Wakhan. As some of the local officials are interested in the trade they do not display much activity in its suppression. In its passage to Chinese territory the opium traverses the Roof of the World, being convoyed by Kirghiz, hardy nomads whose lives are largely spent at an altitude higher than the summit of Mont Blanc. From the world's roof it would pass across the plains of Turkistan and thence into China proper, and so to the East, a journey of several thousand miles, and may, as in the case of the Russian article, ultimately figure in a police court case in London.

CHINA AND THE FAR EAST

CHAPTER IX

CHINA AND THE FAR EAST

WHEN Japan, by her victory over China in 1895, and her phenomenal success against Russia ten years later, assumed a dominant position in the Far East, there were visions of a yellow peril to which the gradual awakening of China, then beginning to materialise, gave additional colour. Fanciful writers portrayed Asiatic hosts sweeping across the Continent into Europe, carrying all before them. It was to be the challenge of Asia, and a glacier-like movement that would crush all obstacles and bring far-reaching changes in its wake.

The spectre was not easy to dispel, but a slight analysis would have softened the picture into less ominous tints. Quite apart from the fact that a combination between Asiatic peoples is hedged around with difficulties of faith, of language, and of social, economical, and political beliefs so widely different and so antagonistic, even were it within the field of practical politics, the time required for such a transition, and to reconcile conflicting interests, would be the work of generations, with inevitable splits as Asiatic history has so amply demonstrated.

It is none the less a fascinating subject, especially in view of the fact that Asia once dominated the greater part of Spain when the Moors appeared there in the seventh century and carried all before them, whilst the

Eastern strain in the character and bearing of the Russian people is evident. Napoleon remarked with conviction that if you scratch a Russian you find a Tartar ; the proof of the dictum is borne out in the Russian music with its Asiatic atmosphere, and in the setting of a Muscovite theatre and its plays, and the general Asiatic tendency.

Change there has been in the Far East, but no sign of aggressiveness such as to constitute a great yellow movement against the West. The evolution has been slow ; in the case of Japan it was certainly rapid, although it is not easy to dogmatise on that question, since Japan had for years remained enclosed and showed no sign of the evolution going on. It grew up like a mushroom in the night, so far as the Western world could see ; the old divine principles of autocracy and the nobility of Japan were largely set aside, and in their place was moulded a political organisation on European lines, with an army modelled on the Prussian pattern, and a navy on that of Great Britain.

The new nation, entering the arena of world politics with its successful war against China, cast around for an alliance, and report has it that Germany was first approached because from her dominant position on the Russian frontier, and her formidable fighting machine, it seemed as though she would be the foremost authority in Europe. On the other hand, there was the United States with its great financial, industrial, and economic resources, and the probability that she would become the paramount Power in the Pacific. At any rate, Great Britain, whether approached first or last, concluded an

Anglo-Japanese alliance, being renewed by periods of seven years until its discontinuance in 1921.

Much has happened since those days ; but there has been nothing to indicate that Japan contemplates any such fantastic inroad as sensationalism would have had us believe. On the contrary, she is engaged on consolidating her position in the Far East, in acquiring trade, and carrying out an extensive programme of industrial development. There is as yet no desire for land conquest, apart from the Pacific littoral ; the Japanese dislike emigration, are averse to moving even to places within their own country, and are essentially a homeland people. Doubtless, in course of time, this will undergo modification as population increases,· which it is doing at the rate of 700,000 per annum, but for the next three to four generations Japanese home and colonial territory are adequate for her needs.

By some Japan has been regarded in the past as a potential danger-wave against the West, due to her relatively small size, the ever-increasing population, and rapidity of growth, but an examination of her human and natural realities dispels that idea. She has quite sufficient in hand with new problems always arising in the growing complexity of modern political and social existence.

Instead of an aggressive tendency towards Europe, we shall see a great development in Japanese industries and trade ; indeed, Japan is now better placed and much wealthier than in pre-war days. With each of the three wars in which she has been engaged Japan has emerged stronger and more united, whilst the national debt has been reduced more than any other Power, and large commercial profits are now invested in European securities.

Another subject akin to the yellow peril is that of Pan-Islamism, or a confederation of the Moslem races, an idea that originated with the nationalist movement in Asia many years ago. It was taken up by the Party of Union and Progress in Constantinople, on the principle that Turkey, and the races in affinity to her, must assert themselves. As it affected Central Asia and Western China I came in close contact with the movement, my investigations covering a wide area and embracing some of the most fanatical sections of Moslem life. They led me to the conclusion that an alliance of Moslem States, divided as they are by religious and national differences, is most unlikely of fulfilment, and there is scant possibility of its becoming a serious menace. Even were such a combination to materialise it would inevitably bring together the white races in solidarity against the danger.

An attempt on a small scale to form a Moslem confederation was made a short time since by Afghanistan, for the present Amir, who succeeded his father in 1919, desired to pose as the champion of Islam and appear well before Moslems. The States of Bokhara, Khiva, and the semi-independent Ferghana, in Central Asia, were sounded with a view to forming a confederacy, the machinery of government, civil, military, fiscal, and judicial, to be at Kabul as the controlling centre. This marked an important era in Asian history, for it was the first tangible step towards Pan-Islamism, but the idea was not well received, the basic reason for its cold reception being the politically independent factors dividing the various Moslem races and sects, amongst whom jealousy, intrigue, and conspiracy are rife.

The Pan-Islamic idea is by no means new ; in antiquity it is as old as the faith itself, but its first modern and practical impetus came during the war, when Germany adopted it as a means of undermining British power. Prior to that she had moulded the original Turkish movement on up-to-date lines, declaring herself in sympathy with Moslem ideals,. and certainly had hopes of disposing of a considerable force in Asia. In the end, those dreams were dispelled, and then the Bolsheviks appeared and took it up to further their campaign for the so-called " Emancipation of the East." They imagined it an easy matter to form such a combination, entirely neglecting the opposing principles. Before it could eventuate Moslems would have to attain a cultural and political-economic level which would secure their political future and safeguard them from aggression. The Islamic world is conscious of this, and the necessity of reform, but much time must elapse before it can effect the mental metamorphosis and transform itself for such a step.

Change in Asia and the Far East is slow, the general trend of the Oriental mind being against haste ; they are people of infinite patience, content to wait indefinitely in the fulfilment of an object. Then again there must be a change of ideals ; Western ideas are being imitated, but to profit from the political wisdom of Europe and America they must inculcate the theory and practice of administration, commercial integrity, and similar secrets of Western predominance. There are other keynotes to strike, truth, confidence, and honesty in all dealings, especially of a commercial nature. Amongst Oriental merchants frequent breaches of good faith occur; we have seen the travesty of justice in Chinese courts, and a general disregard that the fabric of society rests on confidence, justice, and a square deal, whether in a court or a shop.

These, and such as these, must be the ideals of any combine that ambitious Orientals may contemplate.

I will now comment on a matter of outstanding interest, directly concerning the Far East and China. This was the recent reputed *rapprochement* of the Buddhist and Moslem religions in Asia for general action, but primarily intended as a move against India. Being regarded with misgiving, I was directed to inquire into, and report with all urgency on, this fancied menace. I must admit that from the outset it never impressed me as a potential danger, for apart from the fact that an alliance between these rival faiths is impossible, after an analysis of their respective principles and precepts, even were it within the bounds of practicability, the period of transition to a common level of life and thought and being would take generations. They would have to discard their antagonisms, cast off beliefs handed down to them through the centuries, and reconstruct the entire social and political fabric in order to carry out such an alliance.

It was said that the King of the Hedjaz had deputed a representative to Urga in Mongolia, the seat of the Living Buddha and one of the triumvirate in the Buddhist hierarchy. He was to co-ordinate the work of both sides, to act as the liaison officer in this fantastic scheme, and to be the link welding the union together.

A MONGOL CHIEF

THE FRONTIER GUARDS MAINTAINED BY THE CHINESE ON THE
PAMIRS, OR " ROOF OF THE WORLD," ARE MOUNTED ON YAKS
The only cavalry of their kind in the world.

Karakoram, to the north-west of Urga, now in ruins and the object of archæological research, was the ancient capital of the Mongols, and from it a chain of stations was to extend across Asia to Samarkand in Russian Turkistan, once famous in Mongol history and containing the tomb of Timurlane, their most formidable leader, who dethroned no less than twenty-seven kings and even harnessed kings to his chariot. These two main stations had the halo of romance over them; each was invested with a certain sanctity.

The scheme has not materialised; it never could, for Moslems and Buddhists do not fraternise, and an atmosphere of hostility characterises relations between the opposing religions. It is true that satisfaction was expressed at the Japanese victory over the Russians in 1905, but it is traceable to the hostility created by Russia in her treatment of Chinese and Moslems alike in the Far East and on the Asiatic Continent generally. The Japanese were misled by the display of goodwill, and, both secretly and officially, endeavoured to gain touch with Turkey for reciprocal action against Russia, but the efforts were fruitless.

In pursuance of instructions I made exhaustive inquiries, the result of which was to confirm the view already expressed as to the fallacy of the report.

Although there is little to apprehend from any purely Moslem combine, danger threatens from individual sections. This leads us to Bolshevik activities and the strenuous efforts to destroy British power and eliminate our influence in the East. To gain a clear insight into their machinations it is necessary to take a survey of

Central Asia, the political and strategical importance of which is widely recognised.

In pre-war days Russian activities in that region caused us alarm, but they did not aim at world revolution—conquest, and expansion of the Muscovite empire were the goal.

To-day, Central Asia and China have far greater significance, for it is from Tashkent in Asiatic Russia that the Bolsheviks intended to conduct the campaign against India. They declared the success or failure of their schemes must depend upon the results achieved in India, and that this was the only way to ensure revolution in Britain. At the moment the centre of agitation has been shifted, for having failed, temporarily at any rate, in Central Asia, they have seized upon the crisis in China, and the Yangtse Valley in particular, as the new base from which the original object may still be gained.

Let us, therefore, examine the machinery for revolution as it exists in Central Asia, since it forms an integral part of the whole. Ethnographically Central Asia is full of interest and tells us much of the world's history, having been traversed and conquered by successive leaders, both ancient and modern. It consequently has material that might be moulded to the Bolshevik way of thinking.

The Soviet settled on Tashkent as the centre from which to launch the campaign for universal strife, being the most suitable. As the capital of Russian Central Asia it is one of the largest cities in the empire, a granary and supply ground of first-class importance, and an ancient seat of Moslem learning and culture. West of Tashkent lies the Near East and the Caucasian States, to the east China and Mongolia, and to the south India and Afghanistan, altogether a fitting location for G.H.Q. in the renewed campaign for Asian revolution.

A special department for propaganda and instruction therein has been set up in Tashkent. This new element in peace and war has been highly developed by the Soviet, whose founders took it up vigorously in the Russo-Japanese War, when all classes were affected by its disintegrating influence.

Schools have been established, and representatives from the races and tribes of Asia selected to undergo a course in the principles and practice of Bolshevism, with the benefits to be derived therefrom, special stress being laid on the part Great Britain has always played in the degradation of the human race.

The schools are staffed by Russians and natives of proved ability, assisted by a motley collection of Indians attracted to Tashkent to fill the rôle of trained agitators. When the pupils are thoroughly soaked in Bolshevism they are sent out to spread the new " gospel."

In addition to the schools a number of propaganda trains has been formed, fitted with kinema apparatus for showing the alleged horrors of our rule in India and the extent to which the British yoke is pressing upon all Oriental peoples. They are equipped with literature to meet the requirements of the various races, all are catered for, whether Kirghiz, Sart, Afghan, Mongol, or Turkoman. Trained spokesmen, with a fluent grasp of the vernacular, discourse much false and irrelevant matter to their native audiences, and prepare the way for the fiery demagogues of Moscow. The trains comprise

.15

dining and sleeping cars fitted up for the revolutionary staff, who certainly do not believe in forgoing luxury and creature comforts.

To inflame the Asiatic mind many interesting libels have been circulated concerning ourselves, as is now being done with intensified venom in China. It was asserted that the Prophet's tomb at Medina had been bombarded, that we had destroyed the holy places, and cast the Koran amongst swine, whilst we were characterised generally as bloodthirsty exploiters.

In their plans the Bolsheviks consider that by a general conflagration in the East the British can be burnt out of India, and the world revolution can then continue unchecked. At the same time there is method in their madness, for they appreciate the dangers involved in an 'Asiatic flare and realise that only by continually directing its force against the British can they prevent its turning and burning themselves.

The Bolshevik cause in China, no less than Central Asia, derived great strength from the capture of Bokhara and the wealth of its Amir. As is well known, Bokhara is the oldest Moslem State, and its rulers had amassed vast sums which were left lying in the vaults and never invested. To secure the safety of his riches the Amir offered to confide it to our care, the sum totalling £35,000,000 in gold and silver coin and ingots. It was a remarkable tribute to British integrity, but for several practical reasons we were unable to do this, and so the wealth of the Bokharan Amirs remained in its vaults, ultimately becoming the prey of the Bolsheviks, who left no stone unturned to secure it.

The above are some of the preparations carried out in Central Asia, and we now have the operating centre moved to China in general, and Canton, the Yangtse Valley, and Shanghai in particular. It has been abundantly proved that the violent anti-foreign agitation is due to Bolshevik influence, and the Soviet Press congratulates itself upon results hitherto achieved. By a resolution of the Communist International members and adherents in all countries have been called upon to aid to their utmost the world revolution in Great Britain and China. That there is a genuine national feeling in China, admittedly on a small scale, there can be no doubt, but the legitimate aspirations of the Chinese are being exploited for the revolutionary aims of the Bolsheviks. The establishment of the political bureaus at Canton, Hankow, and elsewhere is evidence of this, and wherever there is ground to foment strife and agitation it is at once turned to account.

The official Soviet organ in Moscow, *Pravda,* recently outlined the organisation and working of the Kuomintang Government of the Cantonese party and the importance of political and economic power in organised labour and the necessity of strikes and boycotts to enforce demands even when at variance with more conservative and saner elements. It is a naïve document and details matters with singular bluntness, leaving no doubt of its purpose. For example, Mr. Chen declared that the end of the boycott would mean a more friendly attitude towards ourselves, but this being contrary to Bolshevik ideas, the statement had to be publicly repudiated.

Labour is being organised in the South on the Moscow model, and Soviet authority is dominant in governmental and party institutions. There are details in which the procedure varies, such, for instance, as the condition that all Government employees must belong to the Kuomintang. This brings into its ranks Chinese of the old conservative type who are not in accord with Soviet aims, and here we see the influence of education and the respect in which it has always been held in China. The Bolsheviks, on the contrary, recruit their party largely from the uneducated masses, admit only a small proportion of intellectuals, and have placed a ban on merchants and traders. Up to the present there has been no development of revolutionary lines comparable to the Russian advance and, both nominally and in fact, power is held by the Kuomintang leaders and not exercised by the party as a whole.

The procedure at the Kuomintang meetings is also taken from Moscow. The assembly first rises and sings in chorus the political maxims of Sun Yat Sen, then the business of the day follows, closing with more singing of a revolutionary character, in which, however, old customs do not play a part as these would interfere with the change being brought to bear on the Chinese worker.

In pursuance of the dictates of the Bolshevik Executive of the Cantonese party many drastic orders have been circulated dealing with formation of unions and industrial matters in general, and in their turn the unions have formulated demands to their respective employers. Of these perhaps the most interesting and original, in the nature and scope of its requests, is that issued by the Chinese employees of the foreign banks in Hankow, now organised as a special union under Red control.

It has been reproduced by the *North China Herald,* the leading journal in the Yangtse Valley and Shanghai. The document is a list of twenty-seven demands which are, for the most part, so absurd that they challenge credulity and would not be reproduced if there were not assurances from the best possible authorities that the authors are by no means perpetrating a joke but take themselves and their wants quite seriously :

(1) No employee can be dismissed unless he has committed malfeasance, nor unless the dismissal is approved by the Union.

(2) The bank shall grant full travelling expenses to those employees who have completed one year's service, and who would resign after one year. Those employees who resign after a period exceeding one year shall receive three months' salary ; after two years, four months' salary, etc.

(3) (Unimportant).

(4) The bank shall not be allowed to close without the authorisation of the Union.

(5) Employees can only be recruited from the Union.

(6) Beyond the fixed office hours all employees shall receive one day's salary for every two hours' work overtime.

(7) All employees shall wear the uniform of Dr. Sun Yat Sen, paid for by the bank (uniform includes overcoat, shoes, etc.).

(8) Medical expenses paid.

(9) Forty days' leave every year (travelling and sickness excluded). In the case of a death or marriage of

their relatives, employees shall be granted one month's leave on full pay. In the case of sickness of an employee indefinite leave on full pay.

Those employees who have not taken 40 days' leave shall receive 40 days' salary (additional). Those who take their leave shall receive full travelling expenses in addition to their pay, etc.

(10) The banks shall be required to create a Provident Fund : employees will deposit ten per cent. of their salary ; the banks will add a sum equivalent and will guarantee a minimum interest of ten per cent. All employees will further be entitled to three per cent. of the net profits of the bank.

(11) Employees will receive $15 monthly (food expenses) and $20 monthly (rent allowance).

(12) On the occasion of the wedding or death of a relative the employee will receive $200.

(13) Employees who have been invalided will be entitled to their full salary for life.

(14) Pension :

> After 20 years' service full salary.
> Between 15 and 20 years' service half salary.
> Between 10 and 15 years' service three-tenths salary.

(15) An employee who has worked in a bank for seven years will be entitled to one year's salary ; after 13 years, two years' salary ; after 18 years, three years' salary, and so on.

(16) Should a bank be forced to close each employee will be entitled to one year's salary.

(17) Married employees shall be entitled to $20 extra (monthly).

(18) Clothes, luggage, etc., belonging to the employees shall be insured by the banks.

(19) The above stipulations do not cover those banks

which are willing to grant to their employees still better conditions.

(20) The Union has the right to alter the present rules whenever it thinks advisable to do so.

(21) The banks must accept the demands of the employees if the Union is of the opinion that they should be granted.

Baleful Conveniences.

(22) Employees shall be allowed to request the banks to abolish or to modify what they might consider as harmful to them ; for instance, heating, electric fans, newspapers, etc.

(23) Native employees are free from all responsibility.

(24) Native employees shall be treated on an equal footing.

(25) Employees cannot be used for other purposes than those for which they are employed.

(26) The above rules shall be enforced from January 1, 1927.

Pay of employees :

Minimum salary taels 67.

Employees at taels	10	increase of taels		57
,,	10 to 25	,,	,,	56
,,	26 to 40	,,	,,	55
,,	41 to 55	,,	,,	54
,,	56 to 70	,,	,,	54
,,	71 to 85	,,	,,	52

Increase of pay : Taels 10 (monthly) once a year (minimum). Apprentices will draw taels 30 (monthly) with an annual increase.

(27) On the occasion of every half-yearly balancing of the books all employees will be entitled to three months' extra pay.

(28) Twice a year (end of June and December) they will receive one month's extra pay.

From this it is clear that the banks are to operate by grace of the Union. Events in the Yangtse Valley are being reproduced in Shanghai and other towns and cities ; once Nationalist control is gained Labour demands are increased to impossible standards, factories closed, and the managers imprisoned to force them into signing agreements giving the workers control of factories, and in all cases the demand is made that no employee be dismissed without consent of the Union, which limits the right of management.

Since the Russian Soviet is dominating Cantonese policy and its Press is urging the vital importance of a Chinese victory against the British, coupling with it the determination to render assistance in any shape or form to that end, we reach another matter of paramount interest—the importation of arms into China, a traffic in which the Russians hold the leading share. This illicit commerce with various Chinese military factions in the Republic, and its wide ramifications, render it essential that the facts should be given.

With the close of the war, and spread of disaffection amongst the more belligerent races of Asia, with the impulse given from Moscow, the traffic in arms became an attractive proposition. This applied with peculiar force to China, where the fighting sections offered a constant market, and the problem of piloting the cargoes of arms and ammunition across the land frontiers of China in the north and west presented no serious obstacle.

But it was by no means confined to the land ; the arms came by sea, and to such proportions did it swell that, on the initiative of the United States Minister at Peking, it was proposed by a number of the Powers to ban the export of arms to China. In pursuance of their deliberations an agreement was arrived at in 1919 by which Great Britain, the United States, France, Spain, Japan, Russia, Portugal, and Brazil undertook to prohibit the export to, or importation into, China of arms, munitions, and war material generally, including material for their manufacture, until such time as a Government could be formed competent to act for the country as a whole. The agreement was to apply to contracts for arms and material already concluded but not actually delivered, to which, however, Italy took exception, for consignments of Italian arms were then *en route* to China and were eventually delivered to sundry war lords, action that still further aggravated the situation.

Moreover, under the Treaty of Versailles it was enjoined that Germany should not export arms and war material to foreign countries, yet an examination of the Customs returns for 1924 shows that some 32 per cent. of the arms traffic to China was conducted by Germans.

There were serious flaws in the agreement between the Powers banning the traffic ; it was vague and indefinite regarding machinery for the manufacture of war material, with the result that a great deal came in that was not strictly speaking legitimate, or could be adapted for the purposes of evading the Customs. This was done with the connivance of the war lords, and quantities of material were brought in under various disguises. Then again, there was no provision for aeroplanes and similar material. I have in a previous chapter referred to the air service, which had been organised under British expert advice and assistance for the Chinese authorities in 1919, it being expressly agreed that the new service, and the aeroplanes supplied, should be for commercial purposes only. The Chinese soon disregarded this promise, and the 140 machines, with their equipment, were eventually seized by the militarists.

Notwithstanding the ban there is also a traffic from Japan, whilst French aeroplanes and material have been supplied to the Northern forces, in addition to instructors who are with the latter.

As already indicated, the lion's share in this arms traffic falls to Russia, and the Bolsheviks hold that so long as the policy of disregard and repudiation of treaties is persisted in nothing can happen. Does not their Prime Minister Rykoff say—touching the question of armed force to promote their aims—"we want to make this society a powerful weapon in the hands of our war authorities."

In the passage of arms and war material into China by the land frontiers of Russia and Siberia the matter is simple, for in a region where the line of demarcation frequently follows the crest of mountains, broken up by small valleys and ravines, the task of controlling the inlets is a difficult one in normal times. Vast quantities of material have been recently passed through Mongolia by mechanical transport and caravan, and also by sea to Canton; indeed, there is no pretence at concealment in traversing either the Gobi Desert from the Russian border to just north of Peking, or by the sea route, and owing to the privileged position the Bolsheviks occupy throughout the world with regard to treaties and liberty of action, this brazen trade goes on unchecked.

It has, however, a more subtle and sinister aspect. Payment is not insisted upon in hard cash ; on the contrary, provided an assurance is given that Soviet principles and practice will be followed no monetary payment is necessary, and it can be readily imagined that the importers find no difficulty in securing such promises. Whether they will be redeemed in the future is another matter.

The British Government by a wide system of supervision, extending even to the Central Asian frontiers of India and elsewhere, as well as by sea, has done its utmost to prohibit the traffic, and has also gone so far as to detain foreign ships calling at British ports detected in the act of carrying arms to China.

THE FUTURE OF CHINA

CHAPTER X

THE FUTURE OF CHINA

IN considering the future of China and the Far East generally there are two distinct problems, both complicated and difficult of solution even for those of profound knowledge.

The immediate one is the outcome of the present civil strife and anti-foreign agitation in China. The future of China and her relations with foreign countries are only secondary matters compared with the second problem—the ultimate grouping of the Powers in the Pacific and the vital importance of any readjustment of strength in the new centre of world gravity.

Little has happened in China since 1894 in which a part has not been played, either directly or indirectly, by one or other of the Great Powers.

Our survey of the future, therefore, may well begin by turning to the policies which have dictated diplomatic action in that region.

Foremost herein, since her ambitions aim at hegemony in the Far East, is Japan, whose diplomacy has for years been directed towards that object.

In a previous chapter I have narrated the part played by the Japanese when Yuan Shih Kai was prevented from proclaiming himself emperor. He and Sun Yat Sen are the only leaders of any calibre who have arisen since the overthrow of the monarchy. Had Yuan Shih Kai succeeded in his project of a strong Government it is probable that the present civil war would have ended, for Sun Yet Sen had given him his support. The encouragement, however, by outside influence of an armed rising against Yuan deprived China of the one strong mind left after the overthrow of the Manchu dynasty, and by the chaos thus precipitated, paved the way, *inter alia,* for the Twenty One Demands dealt with earlier in this book.

These demands were modified, it is true, not to placate China, but the European Powers, headed by Great Britain and the United States, who were in favour of the " Open Door " policy. In return for this, and her support of the Allies during the War, Japan secured at the Versailles Peace Conference succession of all rights and privileges in the Shantung province formerly enjoyed by Germany.

China, however, at the invitation of the Allied Powers and the United States, had declared war on Germany, believing that by so doing she would regain Shantung freed from foreign control, and the discovery at the Peace Conference that the German rights were already pledged not to their real owner but to Japan, her ambitious neighbour and rival, exercised a profound impression on the Chinese mind, especially in the democratic South.

Japan and Russia are the two countries which have recently pursued a definite and active policy in Far Eastern affairs, and they are vitally concerned with the outcome of the present conflict in China. Great Britain, the United States, France, and the other Powers

are desirous that China should conduct her own affairs,
and would encourage and assist her to that end so long
as their subjects, interests, and property remain secure.

We have seen the trend of Japanese policy in China
in the Twenty One Demands, the claiming of a zone of
influence in Shantung, her establishment of what is
virtually a protectorate in Manchuria, and her backing,
both by money and arms, the power of Chang Tso Lin,
the Northern war lord. His continued presence in Peking,
indeed, as the virtual ruler of North China, is due to
Japanese assistance afforded a few years ago when part
of his army mutinied and would have captured Mukden,
his capital.

In thus aiding the power of the North, Japan was
pursuing a settled policy of opposition to Russian domination in the Far East, and supporting the Chinese
leader who could be relied upon not to introduce anything
antagonistic to her need of China's raw materials for
Japanese industries, nor jeopardise the Chinese field for
investment of capital and a market for Japanese goods.

Had Japan not strictly maintained the neutral zones
established by her influence and by treaty rights in
Manchuria, and thus to a certain extent protected
Mukden, and prevented the mutinous troops from using
the railways for concentration purposes, the revolt would
have ended with the triumph of the pro-Russian forces
and the sovietisation of China. A scheme had even been
drafted for the incorporation of Mongol territory in the
Urga Republic, a plan which would have brought the
boundary of Soviet Russia to within a hundred miles of
Peking.

The failure of the plan did not by any means dis-concert the Russians ; indeed, as abundantly proved both in the preceding pages and elsewhere, Russian influence has been devoted in China during the past two years in a way hitherto foreign to any sovereign State.

The reason is apparent. With the democratic nations of the West and the great American Republic determined to limit the activities of Russian agitators anxious to stir up class warfare within their boundaries, Asia presents a tempting field for the spread of Communism. Soviet Russia has long been aware of this, and aims at destruc-tion of British, American, and Japanese trade and influence in that part of Asia in which much of the future history of the world is destined to be made.

There were two courses open to the Bolsheviks when they decided upon the permeation of China in the interests of Communism. One was to render their sup-port of the Cantonese open and immediate by despatch of troops to Canton ; the other was to achieve the same result by confining material aid to munitions and instructors, and to trust to a trained corps of propa-gandists to gain the required result—the expulsion of the foreigner as distinct from Russians, and the formation of a Government looking to Moscow for advice and assistance.

The first policy, if adopted, would have precipitated Moscow in a foreign war at a moment when the Russian Treasury was empty, for if Russia had moved Red troops into China or Manchuria they would have fallen foul of Japan as well as Chang Tso Lin. Apart from that, the safety of Vladivostock and the Pacific littoral would have been endangered. Russian interference in Chinese internal affairs may yet result in conflict with Japan, for the latter views with extreme disfavour the activities of Russian agents attempting to inflame China. The collective pressure of the European Powers and America may avert that danger, but the factors behind it will remain. It is not improbable that the first decided check to Moscow's ceaseless propagandist activity in Asia may eventuate through the imperative need to Japan of maintaining her influence in the Pacific.

Japanese statesmen have not forgotten how near Russia came to gaining a great Asiatic empire before the Russo-Japanese War checked her influence in the Far East. The Czars have gone, but Russia remains— a new Russia that turns ambitious eyes eastward as naturally as did the Russia of yesterday.

Apart from this question of the balance of power in the Pacific, there is the subsidiary factor that Russian influence is being thrown into the scale against Japanese interests in China. Should success crown the Russian-inspired plans of the Kuomintang extremists, Japan will lose more than any other nation by the restriction of foreign trade with China. In this economic rivalry Russia has won the first move, for while the Japanese are still unpopular owing to their action in Shantung and Manchuria, Russia is acclaimed by the Chinese radicals as the one power that did not join " the brigand band of predatory nations " who, according to the Cantonese leaders, sought to keep China weak and helpless, industrially and financially, for their own ends.

Next in importance to Russia and Japan in the Far East come Great Britain and the United States.

British-American policy remains that of the "open door" to China, and a neutral attitude in her affairs. At the same time we do not wish to see Russia or Japan securing any form of "protectorate" over one-fourth of the human race during the years while the new China is being evolved. Our interests in the Pacific, and as the greatest naval Power, make it imperative that this ocean shall not become the zone of influence of any one Power. For this reason our policy favours international rather than national action on all questions appertaining to China and the Far East.

With the exception of the United States, British policy during the past few months has been more benevolent than that of any other Power. Although legally justified in refusing modifications, we have waived our privileges at Hankow and Kuikiang, and negotiated fresh terms with Mr. Chen which virtually handed over the British concessions there to the Cantonese. A similar agreement may be expected at Tientsin, and it is probable that in the immediate future, when the Cantonese or other Government can claim to speak for China as a whole, the present concession system, at least so far as this country is concerned, will have passed away, and the former concessions be administered by joint councils of British and Chinese residents. The date of this transfer rests with the Chinese people themselves. As long as a repetition of the incidents following the fall of Shanghai and Nanking in March, 1927, is likely, no Government can agree to withdraw the requisite protection to safe-

A TYPICAL CHINESE CART IN WHICH ONE TRAVERSES THE
IMMENSE DESERTS OF TURKESTAN AND THE PROVINCES OF
CENTRAL CHINA

The cart is springless, and the wheels are studded with large hobnails.

ACROSS THE GOBI DESERT IN SOUTHERN MONGOLIA

guard the lives and property of its nationals from looting, murder, and riot.

Farsighted diplomatists saw that bringing an unprepared China into the Great War was an error, the truth of which time has since confirmed.

By encouraging the Peking Government to withdraw the privileges and concessions enjoyed by treaty rights from Germany and Austria, the Allies raised the question of foreign treaties, jeopardised their position in China, and paved the way for the present attitude towards them.

Even in 1920 we might still have gained Chinese approval and strengthened our position by offering the enlightened reforms contained in the British Memorandum of December 24th, 1926, rather than to have delayed concession to Chinese sentiment in the hope of securing concerted action by all the Treaty Powers. This unity was never, in fact, achieved, and in the end it became necessary to offer a review of the treaties without support from France or Italy, although our policy was viewed with approval by Washington.

Future historians will perceive that had the reforms thus offered to the Chinese nation been spontaneously granted to Yuan Shih Kai, much of the present turmoil might have been avoided.

This revision of British interests in China does not affect our clearly defined position in the Pacific. Great Britain is strong in the southern part of that ocean and weak in the northern. With the surrender of Weihaiwei to China, our one remaining port in the north is Hong Kong, with its magnificent harbour.

Farther south, our new naval base at Singapore will

ensure the adequate protection of British possessions in the Southern Pacific Ocean, including Australia, New Zealand, and Tasmania, in the event of an attempt to promote race rivalry in that area of zealous competition for territorial expansion and influence in the China Sea.

British interests in the Pacific, with the exception of our Chinese trade and the defence of Western Canada, lie south of Hong Kong. North of that port we wish to discourage any advantage being reaped from the chaotic state of the former Chinese Empire, and to protect the lives and property of our own nationals.

The United States, whose influence is outstanding in the Pacific, has for years adopted a similar attitude. Since the Washington Conference, in which China participated, the policy of America has been to encourage China to work out her own destiny, while discouraging any coercion from elsewhere. The fact that the United States marines did not take any part in the manning of the Shanghai defences until after the fall of the city, when it was clear that only armed troops could safeguard American citizens in the international settlement from the mobs without, is evidence of America's determination not to dominate China by force.

This policy is the more admirable when America's interests in the Pacific are examined. Partly because of the danger of widespread Japanese migration to her Pacific seaboard, and also in view of grave doubts regarding Japanese designs on the integrity of China during and after the war, the United States has regarded the Pacific as a vital spot in her world influence since the opening of the Panama Canal, the construction of which has altered the strategic position.

It will be of interest to sketch the rise of American power and influence in the Pacific and Far East. It really began with the establishment of the United States on the Pacific coast by the settlement of the Oregon boundary question in 1846, followed by the annexation of California in 1848, which step led to direct concern in Pacific and Eastern affairs. In 1869 came the railway to San Francisco, affording rapid means of communication, and, incidentally, a set-off later on to the Suez Canal. Although political progress was marked, commercially there was little advance, for at that time America was passing through a stage of industrial and agricultural development ; this, with the schemes for railway construction, absorbed attention to the exclusion of foreign affairs.

Moreover, it was the settled policy of the Cleveland administration from 1893-97 to regard both Pacific and Far East as beyond the American purview.

With the Spanish-American War of 1898 events took a decided turn ; the United States by its acquisition of the Philippine Islands became a colonial Power, new politics and probabilities were· opened up, direct touch was gained with the Far East, and a formidable American outpost was established in the Orient. The strategic advantage cannot be gainsaid ; the Chinese coast was brought within a day's steam, that of Japan within forty-eight hours, whilst geographically the United States is at the cross-roads of commercial traffic between the continents of Europe, Asia, Australia, and America.

Thus did the United States enter the Far Eastern arena, and acquire the principal key to commerce in the Pacific, with sound strategic advantages.

With ourselves, the United States, Japan, and Russia in the reckoning we see that whatever may happen in China, during the coming ten years, there is little likelihood of any one Power securing a monopoly of influence or territory in the Far East. With the fall of the Manchus there was a danger of China being divided among the Powers, but that has passed. To-day there is no nation strong enough or desirous of enforcing such a policy, while in China itself forces are stirring to life which render such dreams impossible of accomplishment. Even in the improbable event of a war between Japan and the United States, ending in an inconclusive peace and with the United States weaker than at its commencement—a view directly contrary to expert naval and military opinion—Japan would be no nearer territorial expansion at the expense of China, for she would still have to reckon with the growing power of Soviet Russia and the hostility of other Western Powers to such a move, not to speak of China herself.

We may therefore eliminate the possibility of absorption of China into the territory of any nation, European or Asiatic. On the contrary, we may expect the balance of power in the Far East to swing slowly against Japan as the influence of America becomes stronger and the period of weakness in China passes. Were the Japanese to challenge this gradual evolution of history in the Pacific, the result might be to endanger their prestige in that region, and even to destroy that of the Mikado, pave the way to overthrow of the Japanese monarchy, and the rise of a radical element which would inaugurate a policy similar to the present phase in China.

What will be the position of China during the coming years ? I think the period of discord will pass away, and China slowly gather strength as her trade and resources are developed by a strong Government with the assistance of the scientists, experts, and finances of the West.

The indispensable factor at the moment is the rise of a leader of capacity, and one imbued with the highest ideals. Hitherto China has lacked disinterested leaders.

The recovery of China will not be rapid. A strong public opinion must precede it to support whatever Government is in power. Looting mobs, uttering the cry of driving out the imperialists, are no substitute for a well-informed public opinion able to wisely support the policy which is in the best interests of China. That public opinion is slowly growing, and is a factor to be reckoned with in the future. It is, indeed, the sole stable source of power behind the Cantonese successes, which can only be maintained in the long run by the popular approval of the educated and business classes of the country.

Another factor to be considered is that, while the history of China shows the rise and fall of dynasties, the social life of the country goes on without check and almost unchanged. When the present civil war has ended it is improbable that one-half per cent. of the population will be conscious of either loss or gain through over fifteen years of fighting. The looting or burning of the international settlement at Shanghai, had the Defence Force not prevented it, would have meant a greater loss to the Chinese masses than the depredations of rival armies, which in China have always lived on the population.

Regarding the form of Government likely to hold power in China, we are faced with three possibilities. Ruling out, for reasons which I have outlined, that of foreign intervention, the civil war may result in (1) the entry of the Cantonese forces into Peking, the diplomatic capital, and the spread of their authority throughout China ; (2) the reinforcement and final victory of Marshal Chang Tso Lin and the anti-Red Generals of the North, who are still—nominally, at any rate—supporting the Central Government at Peking against the Southern "rebels" ; or (3) a "stalemate," with China divided into two separate republics—a "South" with influence extending to Hankow and Shanghai, with the Yangtse River as its northern boundary, and a Northern republic with capital at Peking, and its chief trading ports at Tientsin and Weihaiwei.

The position at present favours the last of these alternatives, always assuming that Chang Tso Lin maintains his opposition to Bolshevik influence in China, and for that reason declines to conclude an armistice with the Cantonese Government. This is assuming a great deal where China is concerned, for, as the last few months have shown, the Chinese are adepts at staging a decisive battle and then allowing one side or the other to gain their ends by bribery rather than fighting. If the story of the negotiations preceding the collapse of both

Sun Chuang-fang and Chang Chung-chang at Shanghai are repeated farther north, then the Cantonese, in the absence of real opposition, may control Peking by the end of the year.

A forecast of future events, therefore, is dependent upon the attitude of Chang Tso Lin, the one leader who up to the present has steadily declined to treat with the Cantonese, and who can probably count on Japanese support so long as he maintains that attitude.

A further factor is the possibility of a serious '' split '' in the ranks of the Kuomintang party itself. As I have shown, the latter is now definitely divided into two wings—Right and Left. At the moment the extremists are in the saddle, but in the event of the Cantonese control of all China none can say how long it would be before the saner elements seized power and put a term to Soviet domination in their councils. Should this occur, the way would be open for an alliance between Chang Tso Lin and the moderates of the Kuomintang, headed by Mr. Chen, for both North and South are now in agreement regarding foreigners and foreign privileges in China. The only outstanding question is whether Mr. Chen's policy of negotiation with foreign Powers is to hold the field, or the demands of the extremists for forcible eviction of foreigners be acceded to. At Hankow the policy followed was a mixture of the two. At Kuikiang the concession was handed over after negotiation ; at Shanghai terrorism was resorted to, and the world has the curious spectacle of the extremists inaugurating a reign of terror against foreigners, while the moderates of the same party endeavoured to suppress them and leave the future of the international settlement in abeyance until peace had once more been restored.

Both North and South are united on the question of "redeeming" China from the foreigner, as is shown by the recent declarations of representative leaders on both sides.

Thus, Dr. Wellington Koo, former Prime Minister of the Central Government, and for some time Chinese Minister in London, stated recently in a message to the *Daily News*: "The régime of special privileges for foreigners in China has generated a deep-rooted grievance in Chinese minds. This régime must be removed, and the urgent importance of the question cannot be over-estimated. A new basis for China's relations with foreign Powers must rest on the principles of equality and mutual respect for each other's territorial sovereignty and sovereign rights."

The former Northern Prime Minister concludes this forecast of the intentions of the Peking Government by saying "the Chinese wish the British Government would see its way to open negotiations on a more comprehensive scale for the revision of existing treaties than is possible in the present limited piecemeal manner."

Compare this declaration, which represents the avowed policy of the Peking Government, with those of Mr. Chen and other Cantonese leaders, who aim to "win back the concessions," not by force, but by what they consider lawful means—*i.e.,* the fomenting of strikes, boycotts, and disorders, rendering trade impossible—and it will be seen that whichever emerges the victor

ᵉ "revision of existing treaties" mentioned by Dr.
ellington Koo will mean, in practice, the virtual dis-
pearance of the concessions as governed in China
·day.

An idea of the future of British and foreign property
ιy be gleaned from the experience of occupiers of
ᵉ former British concession at Hankow, since the
reement abrogating British privileges in that city was
ɲned.

At Hankow the Chinese, after agreeing to accept
ːee seats on the council governing the former con-
ssion area, afterwards demanded the majority, thus
ιcing the control of a section of the city built up by
ːitish enterprise and capital, and with an important
ːeign population, in the hands of a Chinese majority.

view of past and present experience, we could not
ːpect improvements or the maintenance of roads, health
rvices, and sound municipal government under such
ɲnditions.

If a *modus operandi* can be evolved for government
 the concessions by joint councils of foreigners and
hinese, and the question of extra-territoriality can be
 ːttled without leaving British subjects at the mercy of
 corrupt police service and prisons that are a byword,
do not anticipate that China will adopt unwise measures
ιch as wresting the Customs service from the present
ːritish control, or repudiation of external debts.

As soon as the Cantonese either complete the conquest
f China, or realise the impossibility of doing so, and
est content with that portion of the country which they
ιow occupy, we may find conditions slowly returning

to normal, with a steady decline in the influence of Moscow.

It is safe to predict that Communism will obtain little hold on the mass of the Chinese people. Its principles interfere with private trade, which is vital to the Chinese, whilst they strike at private liberty, and we have seen what a strong point that is in social life. To create a communistic spirit there must be certain elements with which to build up the fabric; a republican atmosphere is also difficult to introduce. The component parts are lacking in the national temperament, and until they arise there can be only one form of rule, and that an oligarchic one. In my dealings with the Chinese I have always noticed the consistent respect shown for authority, especially as embodied in the monarchy. With a republic many Chinese argue that there must necessarily be a change of leader, this in itself investing the head of the nation with transitory power and one without prestige, whilst the strong conservative element considers it lacking in the main feature of imperialism, as the term is understood in China, that of concentrating authority and focussing the loyalty of the people.

There will be a period of transition both for the Chinese and for foreigners. A country that is uneducated in a political sense is to vote on policies which it does not understand, and may soon be asked to view the spectacle of a divided China with rival Governments at Peking and Canton, each unable to overthrow the other.

How will the mass of Chinese people regard this spectacle of two Chinas after four thousand years of a compact Empire? Doubtless they would view it with comparative indifference, while along the Yangtse the raids of rival armies would matter little to either side.

Whatever form it takes, the approaching transition period, before the rise of a new stable Government, will prove a trying one for foreigners. The unconditional return of the concessions, if forced upon us, will seriously handicap trade for the next seven to ten years, and the added uncertainty regarding the future will hamper at every turn those dealing with China.

The nations in the days immediately ahead, who prove their friendship and regard for Chinese freedom and national aspirations, will reap the reward to be found in the new China that emerges from the present chaos.

The new nation will evolve slowly, and nine-tenths of it will be a replica of the old. The remainder, the governing part, will be an awakened China intent on learning and applying the scientific and industrial wisdom of the West, a vast and potential market for British and American enterprise and capital, which can offer us not only commercial reward, but the friendship of a quarter of the human race.

The industrial needs of China are many. The factories of the world could work at high speed for the next generation, manufacturing goods for China alone, without raising the standard of living of the individual Chinese to that of Portugal. That is now the measure of the world's opportunity, and its responsibility in China. Under wise leadership the story of Japan may be repeated on a scale surpassing anything yet recorded in history.

There are, however, dangers to be overcome before that stage is reached. We, on our part, have to maintain the trade so carefully and laboriously built up, while pacifying a nation that is expanding and may at times become intractable during the process.

There is, too, the danger that before China has found her strength some cataclysm may occur in the Pacific and rob her of the reward of her efforts. The strengthen-ing of the militarist party at Tokio might stay the Chinese desire for a nation, powerful and free, and possibly convert a part into a Japanese protectorate. The east-ward sweep of Soviet Russia might develop on similar lines, whilst the continuance of anarchy in China itself would, with its repercussion on adjacent States, if prolonged indefinitely, force the civilised Powers to intervene for the sake of China herself.

Assuming the continued supremacy of the white races in the Pacific, headed by Great Britain and the United States, and given the rise of a great leader in China, then the worst of the present chaos will be but the step-ping stone to a new future for the world's oldest empire.

A greater China may emerge, moulded equally of the ancient ethics, the patience, and now the newly arisen zeal for Western science and education. If they will learn and reform, profiting from the experience and modera-tion of the West, the contribution which the Chinese can make to peaceful progress and prosperity of the world will be apparent when they take their place in the comity of nations.

MAP OF CHINA

INDEX

CPSIA information can be obtained at www.ICGtesting.com
Printed in the USA
BVOW08*1048200814

363585BV00017B/360/P